Are You Ready For Civilization Collapse?

Or Are You Prepping For The End Of The World Or When The SHTF Like Some Doomsday Preppers?

Book 1

Peter LeGrove

Who Will Benefit
From This Book

This book is about the future and how to survive it if your world suddenly collapsed. This book is for people who are concerned about where our society is heading. People who want to do something just for a little peace of mind. Just in case things go from good to bad in a very short time.

With the internet, information is just seconds away and now there are always scare stories flying around in cyberspace. This book is for people who wonder whether some of the stories are true. It will give you the confidence to do something that will make a difference without disrupting your life. It adds on to your existing life. Your neighbors will not even know you are preparing for the future.

This book will give you ideas you can put into action. Like building a cache of food storage supplies, that you can use and restock as needed. And what to do if the electricity goes off for an extended period of time. It is not about setting up solar panels and windmills so you are self sufficient in suburbia. It is more about being sufficiently stocked up with food and invisible to people living around.

The ideas put forward are not going to cost you a small fortune to set up. You can set things up over time. I don't think the world is going to collapse in a big rush tomorrow. Preparing for the future is a type of gradual process that you can build on. It is also about information. Information that is invaluable when you need to survive the shutting down of civilization.

The weakest link in our civilization is electricity, and when it goes away we go from The Modern Age to The Middle Ages in a very short time.

How To Use This Book

This book is about doing some new things, possibly for you, but your grandparents would have thought nothing about doing them. Things like turning your backyard into a garden. Then preserving and storing the vegetables, when you have to many. It is about trying new things, like trying to live without the fridge. It is about drying your excess vegetables to store them, and drying meat. Just so you know how to do it, just in case you need to.

The book talks about food storage, but it doesn't give you a list. You have to make up your own list and buy what you think you need. But it does tell you what to look for in a product. It sets your thought processes in motion, so you can live with less without disrupting your life.

To get the most out of the book just read it. Then think about it. Then when you think maybe some spare food would be a good idea. Start buying extra food and putting it in a rotation system, so you eat the oldest food first. I'm not turning you into vigilantes. I'm just getting you prepared just in case your world suddenly comes unglued.

When introducing new things to your family, just start small and do one at a time. Like stocking up on food. Buy a bit extra each week, and try and change the eating habits of your family. Like introducing tinned fish, if you don't already eat it. Then start the garden.

This book will help to answer the question "Maybe?" If you are a little bit worried about the hyperinflation stories, and need to get on top so you are in control. Then this little book is the blueprint. You can look at your situation, and start to do things like doing something about water. What do you need to buy to survive if the supermarket shuts down or get looted? What about vegetable seeds, how many do you need. To be honest you need lots especially if you are going to live off sprouts for any length of time.

About Me

Hi, I'm not one of those survivalist, psycho nuts, who think the whole world will be against them when their little world comes unglued. Stocking up with the big guns, and holing up in some wilderness hideout, waiting for the end. Mind you I do watch the TV programs, but I believe in society and community. And I think that is where the future lies.

I'm Peter Legrove, just your everyday dude, who has taken a liking to the looming crisis that could be the end of the world, as we know it. I'm like most people my age, did the scout thing when I was younger. Got pretty good at it and could crash out in the wilds, for a while, without too much trouble. Anyway after I started working I was a volunteer for the Red Cross Disaster Relief. That was a good weekend thing to belong too. And we got to go to a few disasters, mainly floods, but usually we just went to sports events. A lot of fun, but not serious stuff. Except for the floods. There we got to see the real stuff, and helped out quite a bit. Years later, like a few years ago, it dawned on me. If there was no outside help coming in, the people caught up in the flood would be in some serious trouble.

Well somewhere between then and now, I joined the Peak Oil craze that morphed into the Global Warming crisis, and now all seems to be forgotten. So something is bound to happen soon. And that is what worried me so much that I starting looking into how to come out the other end still intact. And this book is the result of what I found out.

I used to live in Asia, and there most of the food is grown close to where it is eaten. So they have a distinct advantage and food is cheap. In the West where food is expensive, very few families have a garden. They still rely on the government. I have a garden and I'm into drying the excess and simple preserving. My sister has the chickens and the bees, so hopefully between us we should come out the other end, still intact.

With shopping we buy stuff that can be used and reused. We look at food in containers to see if we can use the containers. We are not trying to reshape our environment, just change to do things and buy things that will help to keep us alive when all around us is wondering what happened.

This book is the end result of my seven years of wondering and doing something, to be ahead of the Peak Oil and Global Warming mess that should involve us in the very near future. When I give up waiting for the future, something will happen so I am still waiting, and somehow I think the wait is nearly over.

Table of Contents

Documentaries, Books and Magazines Mentioned

Movies That May Have Influenced This Book

The Future Will Be Here Sooner Than You Think

All The Best For The Future.

What You Need
To Do
NOW

Chapter 1

What Is Happening Now

It seems inconceivable that our modern way of life is actually on the verge of collapse. But why not? Our history is littered with civilizations that have left behind beautiful decaying cities, where the man made structures have stood the test of time. But the people who inhabited these archaeological wonders, have disappeared into the sands of time. What makes us different? The Roman Empire, one of the greatest empires on the planet, just outgrew itself and collapsed, taking all their technology with them. Why can't we? I look at this beautiful city I live in, and wonder how we can keep getting the energy to power the city. We can't. I can't see our civilization collapsing, mainly because it is all I know, but we can't keep carrying on the way we are. We are running out of nearly everything we need to survive. Water is the big one because we can't live without it. And we need water for food, so when the water goes, so does the food. We can live without electricity, and we can live without oil, but water is life. But we are so dependent on oil and electricity that when we run out, we will go from the Modern Age to the Middle Ages in a very short time. And the Middle Ages supported a lot less people than are alive in the world today.

To survive the future, you have to come to terms with the idea, that the future might not be as rosy as the past. Just before the Roman Empire came to its end, the average Roman citizen could never have dreamed that, in a few short years his whole life would be turned upside down. But even after the Roman Empire collapsed, there were places that were not really affected. They still thought the Roman Empire was the greatest empire on the planet. There was a severe reduction in the number of goods and services, but they were not overly affected. Now there will also be places that will not be too affected by the collapse of our civilization. And it is these places you should gravitate too. But where are they?

Even now in modern times, a 30 to 40 year old Chinese citizen living in a modern city, could never have imagined that they would be living the way they are now. They never dreamed they would own a car, or live in a modern apartment with all the modern trappings of modern society. When they were in primary school or middle school, they could never have imagined the life they are living now. Yet they are, and now they can't even remember life without air-conditioners. But that same generation will see their world collapse, as famines and water shortages affect the planet. On the other side of the coin we can look at Egypt. Since the building of the Aswan Dam in the 1960's, Egypt has had 100% population growth. And anybody living on the banks of the Nile in 2008, would never have dreamed that their country would collapse into chaos, when food became too expensive to buy. But it did and that looks like the future for Egypt, and other countries that have had unregulated population growth. China has had the One Child Policy for nearly 30 years now, and it is heading for superpower status and now they have a two child policy.

When the Roman Empire went under, the technology they invented also went with them. That is the same with all major civilizations. We still don't know how the pyramids were built, or how the statues on Easter Island were moved. Will the archaeologists of the future, figure out how we built the Hoover Dam or the towering skyscrapers of Dubai, after they find this abandoned city sticking out of the desert sands. The empires of Central and South America had more people living in those areas, than live there today. Their rainwater harvesting and storing was a lot more advanced than what is in place today. They survived because they knew the value of rainwater. But modern man relies on electricity to pump the water, and now rainwater harvesting is largely forgotten. Places in India and Africa are now returning to collecting rainwater. Some medical archeologists have suggested that we passed the medical knowledge of the Romans about 200 years ago. That meant for over 1000 years our medical knowledge went backwards. And for us when our civilization starts to crack, our modern medical knowledge will vanish into the sands of time. So the future of your children and grandchildren depends on the choices you make over the next few years. You need community, as we have a better chance of surviving if we stick together. But what community? Cities cannot live without water, oil or electricity, so cities and the surrounding areas could become a danger zone to keep away from. Right now there are many ordinary people and experts predicting the end of our civilization. And they all seem to agree that cities will be overcrowded dog eat dog zones, except all the dogs will be eaten. I expect water borne diseases, like Cholera and Typhoid, to take out large swathes of the city population very soon into the start of the collapse. Just make sure you are not one of them.

The internet has made life incredibly easy for us, and it has also made news more accessible. We are now bombarded with an immense amount of news, and we are exposed to news that before we would never have heard about. So now you would have most likely have heard about the coming collapse of western civilization. Before it was a specialized topic, and the few people interested in the future would read the books and think about them. Now with the internet and blogging, more people are aware of the situation and are wondering about the future. Also experts on collapse, like Gerard Diamond, seem to give the impression that we are heading for collapse. When I was watching the National Geographic "Collapse" program hosted by Gerard Diamond I got the impression he didn't think there was much hope for mankind, and he should know he wrote the book "Collapse". And that program is only set 200 years into the future. So what happens now? We can see the problems around the world. And they are getting worse. We can see the droughts, the bush fires and the wars, as well as the riots caused by food shortages. And we know the situation is getting worse, not better. And to top it off we just passed the 7 billion mark, at the end of October 2011, for the number of people on the planet. A sad day for the human race. Now I think some people are starting to realize that maybe, just maybe there are a few too many people living on the planet. But it is a bit late. Every child born this millennium will have a terrible life, starting very soon. The famines are back with Somalia getting food aid. I think this is the first famine since the Live Aid concert for Ethiopia, back about 30 years ago.

What really gets me is the world is still trying to blame somebody else. In the global warming conference in Dubai, South Africa was blaming the West for climate change and saying how they would be affected. South Africa only contributed a very small amount to global warming. Yet Africa and the Middle East, according to the National Geographic magazine in January 2011, have some of the highest population growth rates in the world. But they could not see the connection between population growth and global warming. A one child family, like they had in China, is going to cause a lot less CO2 over the generations than a two, three or more children family. People cause climate change and resource depletion, yet nobody seems to want to make the connection. It is easier to blame another country than do something yourself.

Now the question you should be asking yourself is: What can I do now to prepare for a future that will most likely not be as rosy as how we are living now? Start planning now. Start a garden and stocking up on food. Try and have a few months of food in your house. Very important, start saving seeds now, you will need them. If push come to shove you can live off sprouts for a while, but you need to have seeds. Also stock up on essentials like antibiotics, rubbish bags and toilet paper. And anything else you think you will need, like hard candies for the kids.

Chapter 2

The Mindset You Need To Survive The 21st Century

The mindset you need to survive the 21st century is all about making the correct choices now when you do anything. If you plan to stay where you are, then start setting your house up so you can still live there, when essential services are no longer available. The most important is rainwater collection because town water is going to go off. Anything that relies on oil and electricity will go off. Put up a big tank to collect rainwater from the roof. It might be an idea to put the tank inside the garage or underground, so it is not visible. You do not want the meandering mobs to be able to see the water tank, because then they will just shift in and kick you out. As happened during the aftermath of Hurricane Katrina.

Most collapse experts all seem to agree on one thing and that is - cities will become uninhabitable. In the cities there will be too many people and too few resources, so it will be survival of the fittest. The takers will just take, so to survive you need to be invisible. And that means you cannot draw attention to yourself, so keep everything hidden. No solar panels on the roof. I would forget about electricity. Solar panels will be like gold. So people will just take them. Solar panels will only last about 20 years then what do you do. So how do you stay invisible in a city where people are watching your every move? First, make you house look like it has been looted. Throw everything you don't need on the front lawn, and leave the front door open so people think, nobody lives there. And hopefully nobody will look inside. If you live in a cul da sac you could block off the road with burnt out cars. If you live in a small town it would be easier to band together with your neighbors to survive. If you decide to stay in the city, you will have to band together with your neighbors, family and friends, just to survive.

The cities will become safe and habitable again, when there is equilibrium between numbers of people and resources like food and water. After the parks, football stadiums and vacant lots are growing vegetables and rabbits and chickens, and there is enough clean water for everybody, then the cities will be all right to live in. But that will take time.

Now back to your house. Once you have the rainwater tank set up start thinking about recycling water. You can start a simple recycling system just by using buckets. Just remember sunlight destroys plastic so keep your plastic buckets out of the sun. I mean don't leave them lying around outside in the sun as people could see them and take them. And after the electricity goes off buckets are probably all you can use. So you need to buy some buckets and start using them. Get into the habit. Now you can use recycled water in the toilet and on the garden, you can even wash your clothes in a bucket and then recycle the water on the garden.

The washing machine is no good without electricity and it uses heaps of water. If you start doing this now, then by the time the problems start to occur, you have in place a system that will keep you alive and well. If solar panels are the gold of the future, then seeds are the currency of the future. So get into the habit of saving seeds. All food you buy that has seeds, just save the seeds. Then throw them around near where you live. In vacant lots, on the edges of parks where the city council doesn't look, on water ways and in places where they will grow. Seeds only need soil, sunlight and water to grow, so anywhere there is soil that will not be disturbed should be okay. Vacant lots should stay vacant for years to come. If you have ever tried to sell a vacant lot you'll know what I mean.

When you are throwing the seeds around, you are trying to start a self-seeding garden. Where the seeds you throw around will grow into plants and have vegetables and these vegetable seeds will grow into new plants. So you know where there will be vegetables plants and apple trees growing when the time comes. There are many types of seeds you can throw around. Admittedly if you want to go all out you can buy seeds and drop them round. Like carrots, radishes, celery, kale and many more vegetables that don't have seeds when you buy them. Kale is amazing if you leave some plants to go to seed there will be kale plants growing everywhere.

To do a practice run growing your own vegetables, start by throwing seeds around the backyard. Don't dig the garden just throw some seeds around and see what comes up. All seeds from the kitchen go into the backyard, so you can start growing your own vegetables. Just check when is the best time to sow the seeds for different crops. In the future there will be no fertilizers, no pesticides, and no herbicides so start without them. Then by the time you can't buy them anymore your garden will be flourishing. To keep the nutrient levels up in your garden, you should get into the habit of throwing all waste vegetable and meat material back onto the garden. I don't use compost I just return all live waste material back to the garden, and this keeps it alive. We call this natural gardening and the ultimate goal is to have an edible meadow where everything is growing together.

Probably the hardest part of getting the right mindset is the waiting. We do not know when the collapse will start, or how many false starts there will be. So you are actually setting everything up just in case. I somehow don't think you will have to wait very long. And then you do not know how the collapse will happen. I think it will be a gradual decline as society slowly breaks down. Or there will be a serious climate weather event, like an El Nino event that slowly destroys parts of the world. But the climax is when the electricity goes off and doesn't come back on again. That will be the end of civilization as we know it. I've been waiting for many years now, and the more I look into collapse scenarios from the past, the more I think the lead up time to collapse takes a while. Then all of a sudden it is here.

Actually good things are happening, like many families are returning to gardening and because of the financial collapse families are spending less. So more people will be prepared when something happens but I don't think anyone, including me is mentally prepared for the amount of death and destruction that will happen. Even the movies and documentaries say very little about what will happen to the people alive when the end starts. I think after any sort of breakdown of society, diseases will run rampant. As soon as the water gets contaminated, there will be cholera and typhoid and that will thin out the population. If SARS comes back then that will also affect the population. I call SARS the wolf of mankind as it only takes out the old and the infirm. The same as the wolves take the old and the infirm from the caribou herds. At present I don't think there is a vaccine for SARS, but I do think it will make a comeback.

Modern man is very fragile as our way of life has made our bodies very weak and people are just going to drop dead over very little things. So you need the will to survive and live just to get through the first couple of months when all around you are collapsing and dying. And that could be your family too. That is why bleach and hydrogen peroxide are so important. You must have safe water to drink. If you are in a very hot climate in the middle of summer and you have no safe water to drink. You are in trouble. If you can get through the first couple of months intact, then there will be less people competing for the few resources that are left. And that is when your planning will pay off. You'll be glad you threw seeds around, as there will be edible plants growing food near where you live. And you have your water tanks so you have safe water to drink. But to have all this you must be able to protect it, so you should be thinking about how to keep your house safe and invisible. Or think about moving? Moving would be very difficult at the beginning of the crisis, so I would hold off until things calmed down a bit. There is a chapter later on about moving and it doesn't involve the car. Also there is a chapter on staying invisible.

Right now we are just getting all the things together that you need to survive the first three to six months. Hopefully by then things would have calmed down somewhat. I'm not into guns, weapons or warfare but I know people who are. So I keep in touch and when things come apart I could ask them to join with us. I'm not thinking about a private army, just a live in consultant who could keep us up to speed on how to stay alive in a battle zone. The main part of survival is preparing your mind. And that is by realizing there could be a problem and preparing for it. Most people don't even think our civilization could come apart but I'm worried about the future. That is why I am doing something about it. I don't think society is going to come apart rapidly in the very near future. I think there will be a gradual decline into chaos so that gives you a bit of time to get prepared. Every time I go shopping, I'm on the lookout for items that will come in handy when things start to deteriorate. Just the other day my wife saw a handy little knife on special so she brought it. Just being on the lookout is a start. There is a problem with a gradual decline and that is you think it will not get any worse and you are doing nothing. Then all of a sudden it is worse and you are too late. As has been said "It is better to be a year early than a minute late when it comes to collapse.'

I would start thinking about a bug-out bag or a 'get out of Dodge' bag or whatever you call it. Just in case you have to make a run for it. Just remember you have to carry it so make sure you can. I'll get into bug-out bags a bit later on. Right now we are starting the thought process. Getting you ready to stock up on food and essentials first then throwing together a bug-out bag. If you buy a bug-out bag make sure you know what is in it, and that means taking it apart and having a look. Then adding and changing things you don't like. I'm stocking up on army pants with lots of pockets so I can carry a lot on me. I don't want to have everything in one bag.

Chapter 3

What You Need To Buy

You must always ask yourself when you buy something. Can I use this without electricity? Is it durable enough to last a long time? Now you have to change your way of thinking. You are not buying things for the present you are buying for the future. So that means quality. And quality means price. There are a few items that you should think about buying now just to get used to using. The most important is the thermal cooking pot. This is like a hot water thermos flask. It works the same way but instead of just keeping the food hot, it actually finishes cooking the food. When you want to cook a soup or a stew just mix everything up in the small pot that fits inside the thermos cooking pot. You can either cook the soup or stew in that pot for 10 to 15 minutes, or you can pour the already cooked food into the pot. Then close the little pot in the thermos part and leave for as long as possible. You can leave it over night if you like.

I usually cook it in the morning and leave the food in the thermos all day, then it is still warm for supper. It needs to stay in the thermos for about three to four hours to be cooked. Also the meat and vegetables should be diced quite small. The vegetables not so much but the meat has to be cut quite small so it all gets cooked. If the meat is not cooked after being in the thermos I will cook it again on the stove. This little cooking thermos saves a lot of energy, as you only need to cook the food for a short time. And when things go from bad to very bad these little thermos cooking pots will come in handy. Also the golden rule is only cook what you and your family can eat in one sitting or two at the maximum, because you wont be able to store food in the fridge anymore. We will assume the electricity has gone off and you have no fridge or stove. So you can't store food. Also when cooking over an open fire, don't cook in the pot that comes with the thermos just to keep the outside clean. Cook in another pot and pour the food into the little pot if you can. I have two of these pots now and I use them a lot. But I can store what is left over in the fridge, and there is always some left over. So don't buy too big a pot. I'm thinking of buying a smaller one just to see if we can empty that in one sitting.

When you are buying cooking utensils always buy good quality steel cooking containers. And I mean all steel even the handles. When you look at pots and pans you will see that some handles are coated with this black stuff that stinks when it is burning. So only buy completely steel handles or half steel half wood, as that will save your nostrils when you are cooking over an open fire or in a fire mud oven. Wooden handles do not get as hot as steel handles. Also wooden handles are not as good as steel as they tend to split. Some pots and pans have a black coating on the bottom, forget those and others have a nonstick surface forget those too.

Look at the quality of the finished product. Look at the rivets and see if they will last a lifetime because they might have too. When buying any cooking utensils or pots and pans look for good quality stainless steel with nothing that can burn or break. Plates and bowls are a bit different, as you can't really have steel plates and bowls on the kitchen table. You can get steel serving bowls so that is a start. When you are restocking the kitchen, just think about the future and how long the things you buy will last, because you might not be able to buy them after the collapse.

Now for clothes I only buy the best quality, I've given up on the cheap goods that are guaranteed to fall to bits. I buy well-known brand name jeans and boots because I know they will last. My white shirts and my long pants for work are still the cheap stuff, but my outdoor clothes are the best. Even my sandals are brand name and they have lasted a good four years, but they are starting to fall to bits now. I've already had to superglue the soles back on. For things like boots, jeans and outdoor work clothes buy the best and you'll be glad you did. I thought about stocking up on little things that make life easy like superglue and duck tape. I do have plenty lying around the house. But I'm still thinking about whether it is a good idea to stock up on things that make life easy now. Then after they run out just make do.

I would also get some spring-loaded rat-traps as rats will be a severe problem after the cities come unglued. Also rats are meat, I've never eaten them but I have seen them on the menu when I was in China, and they are a delicacy. You will need to buy things that will catch food like the spring-loaded rat-traps. I'd also look at buying some good fishing gear. Like hooks, sinkers and plenty of fishing line. A fishing rod is debatable but if you are into fishing, buy a rod or two because you will need to be able to fish when things calm down. If you can fish you can survive, keep that in mind. Buy many sized hooks and many different lines of different strengths, because you do not know what size fish you will catch. Just remember a small hook will catch a small fish as well as a big fish, but a big hook will only catch a big fish so have many small hooks.

Also look at bicycles, as you might need them to get around. But buy a very expensive, very simple design. You don't want a bike with too many moving parts, as there are more parts to break and once they break the bike could be finished. A standard bike with no gears and a couple of good quality chains should be OK. Next stock up on tires and inner tubes and plenty of rubber patches, because after the electricity goes off there will be no more. If you buy two bikes always buy two exactly the same, as this way you will have spare parts. You can use one bike to keep the other workable.

Try and buy a very good sowing set of needles and thread, so you will to be able to mend your clothes. I started darning my socks just to see if I could do it, but I do need a bit more practice. Also try out knitting needles, as you might have to make your own clothes. Now at the moment you don't need these things, but you will when things come unglued.

When society breaks down there will be no more goods coming in. After the Roman Empire collapsed the flow of goods stopped. The Romans had a very good logistic system in place and they could get products from the far-flung corners of the empire onto the streets of the main cities. After the collapse that all stopped and the same will happen here. There will be no more cheap readily available Chinese goods so you will have to make do. I think razor blades would come under the heading of can't do without. If you try growing a beard after the first week it gets really, really itchy. Then after three or four more days it is alright. So look around you and find the things you can't live without and stock up on them. Or now before you can't buy them anymore try to live without them. I am not recommending all the men grow beards, but during your holidays try not shaving and see what happens.

You should start looking at survival equipment but don't go overboard. You'll need a pocket knife, fire starting flint and steel and a few things you have never thought off. I try and buy stuff that you can use around the house and backyard. Like black rubbish bags good for rubbish and also good for keeping dry when out in the wilds. If you have some trees in your back yard tie up a hammock and see if you can sleep in it. Usually in and around your home you have most things you need. Like garden equipment and axes and tomahawks. I would look at buying a pocketknife and a good bush knife or two with a sharpening steel, as well as and a multipurpose tool or two. Stick to what you use now because you are used to using it. When buying survival equipment buy what you think you might need. Don't go out and buy what is the most popular at the moment. You already have most things you need and you are already using them. When buying new stuff to replace something that has worn out then think how long it will last, and buy quality. Buy stuff that is built to last. That will be more expensive but in the long term it will pay off. I gave up buying cheap goods a long time ago. Now I never buy the cheapest I will usually buy something in the middle range.

Barter Items

As society comes unglued money will take a backseat to barter. Real money will be hard to come by and very soon into the crisis will very possibly not be used. There are a lot of people, gurus or whatever you like to call them, saying gold will be the new currency. But in a crisis situation what would you take if you are selling a gun. Cans of food or a one ounce gold coin. Unless you have got plenty of food you are going to take the food. Just recently some of the gurus are saying stock up on $1/10^{th}$ gold coins, which I think are more useful than one ounce coins. But what about for small things you want to barter for. What can you barter for a can of beans. Think small like a cigarette lighter or even tobacco. I don't smoke but I've still brought a couple of cartons of cigarette lighters. I like to have a cigarette lighter on me at all times, after watching the Discovery program "I Shouldn't Be Alive." When ordinary people get lost in the wild, life would have been a lot easier if they had a lighter so they could make a fire. That simple item could have been the key to survival in a lot of situations. And when things start to go from good to bad then I'll stock up on tobacco.

If you can make moonshine you will be set up for life as long as you have your own private army in place to guard you and the still. Marihuana and moonshine will be in demand after food and clean water are catered for. Also if you can make beer you will also be set up because the fermentation process will turn unsafe water into a safe drink. Also this knowledge could very well keep you alive. If you are the only person who can make beer then the meandering mobs will want you alive. Just remember the Roman Empire marched on beer.

Knowledge is one thing that they can't take away so if people know you can do something like make beer or are a doctor then you should be alright. Except the dominant gang will probably try and steal you as well as all your equipment. Actually nearly everything will be barterable so stock up on nearly everything you use now. People always want useful things. I'm always on the lookout for things that will come in handy. The latest little item I brought was a hand crank torch. It looked pretty good and worked alright so I've stocked up. Now I'm after a more expensive model that could work better. Some things will be more valuable than others like guns and ammo. Depending on how dangerous the situation is they will most likely be on top of the list. You will need plenty of ammo and if you can, make your own bullets you will be in demand. Another skill that could keep you alive. Then after you are safe you will need food and that will be a constant everyday thing. Getting enough food and water will dominant your life until your garden is growing. Then you will need to guard it. Seeds in my book are very important so I'd be very careful bartering them away. You might have to live off sprouts for a long time.

After the electricity goes off making fire will be very important so cigarette lighters will be like gold so stock up. Everyday things we use all the time will vanish so stock up. Some people can't do without toothpaste and toilet paper so have plenty on hand. I don't know why but every time I see rubbish bags on special I stock up. Little things like sowing needles and thread, and fishing gear will be on somebody's list to buy. Keep in mind what other people want and stock up. That is why you want to keep a lot of food in your house so you have something to batter. Before battering anything away I'd make sure I have enough for myself. When I'm walking round the supermarket I keep an eye on anything on special saying to myself 'Do we need this' and then I think 'Will anybody else need it' and I'll probably buy it. Now I'm getting good at prices in the supermarket and I know what is cheap and what is not.

Chapter 4

Your Bug-Out Bag

There are a few things you need to consider with your bug-out bag, or your 'get out of Dodge bag' or what ever you call it. The first and most important thing you have to consider is: How heavy is it? Because you have to carry it and that goes for all members of your family. They must be able to carry their own bag. Also you might have to run with it on your back, so have a few practice runs to make sure you can. Make sure all your family's bags are self contained. That means they must be a separate unit by themselves, so if you lose one bag it doesn't really matter. You cannot have the medicine in one bag and the food in another because if you lose one bag you are screwed.

I consider that the most important part of putting together a bag. If it is too heavy to carry you could lose everything if you are on the run. The next most important thing is something to purify water. I prefer bleach and hydrogen peroxide (H2O2) so I carry that. H2O2 can be used as an antiseptic to clean wounds. You will need an eye-dropper to measure the drops when you add bleach and H2O2 to water. Also some cotton buds if you are going to use H2O2 on wounds. You carry what you want to use to clean your water. That is up to you, but you must have something because you are not going to get very far without water. Also one water bottle per bag should be enough to get started. Throw that in just before you leave so it is fresh. Now for food, get packets of beef jerky as they are small. That should keep you going for a while. If the jerky is individually wrapped open the packets and throw it in your bag. And if you haven't got diabetes open a few packets of hard sweets and empty them into your bag as long as they are individually wrapped.

To get food on the run you need something to catch it with. And that means a small fishing kit and some heavy duty spring loaded rat traps as these will catch rats, cats, rabbits and most small animals. Make sure you have wire to tie the trap to a tree or a post. Next up are seeds in moisture proof packets. When you buy seeds buy the packets with the most seeds in them. You will need seeds to start your garden when you get to where you are going. Just throw them in your bag. Next I would throw in a packet of big rubbish bags. Bags big enough to sleep in and to climb in when it starts raining. You do not want to get wet and you can also collect water to drink with them. If you are not into rubbish bags get a poncho and a space blanket. With a poncho you can move around in the rain but with a rubbish bag you usually stay put. Just keep that in mind. Now for your first-aid kit, snake bite kit and sowing kit make sure it has sterilized needles and thread to use as stitching in case you have to stitch up a wound, as well as butterfly bandages. I don't use painkillers so I have no Aspirin or Tylenol but that is up to you.

If you can, put in a thermal cooking pot and or something for boiling water and cooking. The thermal cooking pot has a pot inside you can boil water in, so you don't really need two pots. If you like you can throw in a bowl and a couple of forks and spoons. You need something to start a fire with like a few cigarette lighters, magnifying glass, matches or a flint and steel. A flint and steel and a magnifying glass will outlive the others, so use the cigarette lighters for bartering. These things are the essentials, the rest is what you can carry. On your belt or strapped to your leg you can carry your knife and baton, keeps guns concealed. I like army pants and vests because they have lots of pockets and you can put many things in the pockets. And I would carry most of the essentials in these pockets like bleach and H2O2, and fishing gear. You can buy a couple of sling shots from the army surplus stores and practice with them. And if you are any good throw one in your bag and have a couple of the rubber bands in case one breaks.

If you want to know what is happening out in the world get a hand crank torch, radio combined. If not just a torch. Also I'd thrown in some cord and duck tape as that will come in handy. Especially if you are making a shelter. That is where your big rubbish bags can be used. Last but not least your favorite survival manual and first aid manual. If you can find a hand crank book reader load it up with all your survival pdfs and throw it in. I'm still looking for that so if you find one let me know. Or you could throw in a standard hand crank generator to keep it alive.

Your Bug Out Bag should be set up with the end in mind. If you are running to your little patch of land in the countryside which has all your gear and is already stocked up. Then your Bug-Out Bag will contain what you need to get there and that is about it. If you are running from the city with nowhere to go except where you think is a good place then you will stock your Bug-Out Bag with what you need to start over again. I think it would be better to plan and have a place to go to. This way you will not have to carry too much. If your parents are healthy you could set them up in the countryside with a small place and you could go there. Just a thought.

Chapter 5

What You Should Be Stocking Up

Vegetable seeds in water proof packets. Most seeds are already in moisture proof and mouse proof packets and the use by date is usually pretty good. But you must store them in a very dry place preferable away from sunlight and moisture. In the loft is a good place or if you can among the rafters at the top of your house. There should be a trap door somewhere so you can get up there. Or just hang them up in the garage in muslin cloth, should be OK. It is a good idea to stash seeds and other essentials in different places around your house, garage and garden shed. It will probably be better if you can buy organic seeds or seeds ready for milling. If you are buying farmer seeds or seeds for farming, then these seeds will have insecticide on them to stop the bugs eating them in storage. Be careful with these seeds. Before you put them in the sprouting trays they must be washed and washed good. If you buy seeds ready for milling then they have already been cleaned. When the supermarkets run out of food things will go from bad to very bad very quickly. And that is where your stack of seeds will come in handy. If it is spring or summer you will be okay, just set up a tray of sprouts wait about a week and you'll have something to eat. If it is winter put the trays in a warm room with lots of sunlight and they should grow. Hopefully the electricity hasn't gone off. Some supermarkets sell bean sprouts, they just cut off the sprouts as you need them. You are going to grow the same type of trays in your home. The idea is not to grow too many trays at once. You should try and set up a rotation system using different seeds. It is very easy to get sick of eating bean sprouts all the time. So plant different seeds. Even if you have nothing else to eat a tray of sprouts will last a couple of days.

The idea is not to set up too many trays. You do not want to waste any because when the seeds run out you will have no more food. To conserve seeds you should wait as long as possible before eating. Most sprouts you start eating at about 4 to 6 inches high. I'll try to wait a bit longer to get as much out of the trays as possible. You will need to buy some sprouting trays but you'll only need about 3 or 4 trays. The trays in the supermarket have a thick carpet of sprouts. They look really good and really even. I would try a few practice runs just so you know what you are doing. This way you can rotate the seeds by using up the old seeds and buying new seeds. And you will know how many seeds to put in each tray. Also you will see that you will use a lot of seeds in a very short time so stock up on seeds. All kinds of vegetable seeds. Even big seeds like pumpkin seeds and watermelon seeds as they can be eaten raw. After you buy the trays, put some seeds in one tray add water and see how long they take to grow. Then eat them so you know what they taste like, and get your kids used to eating something that doesn't come out of a packet.

Grow trays throughout the year, so you know how long the seeds will take to sprout in different seasons. You will also realize the value of the seeds and you will look after them. I would also set up some pot plants so I can leave some plants to go to seed so I can restock my seed supplies. This is very important because once you have run out of seeds you have problems. Also vegetable seeds can be used to barter with and big seeds like pumpkin and watermelon seeds can be eaten raw if there is nothing else to eat. So you must replenish your supplies and that means growing plants for seeds.

So What Are The Seeds You Should Stock Up On?

Most people when thinking of sprouts think of bean sprouts, so stock up on the bean seeds. A couple of bags of bean seeds will go a long way. I would also look at alfalfa seeds, and wheat and barley seeds. Any vegetable or crop you can eat, get the seeds. Broccoli sprouts are very good so stock up on broccoli, cabbage, kale and cauliflower. The best is possible alfalfa seeds, because the seeds are very small and you can store a lot of the seeds in a very small area. Alfalfa is not usually a seed crop but the other seeds you can grow into a crop when the world calms down. You should stock up on all vegetable seeds. And if things go from bad to very bad very quickly just start planting some seeds straight into your lawn, don't start digging. Don't throw the seeds around because seeds are very valuable now so don't waste any. Just plant how many you think you and your family can eat. Then a week later plant some more. Plant on a rotation basis, so you have vegetables ready to eat and more still growing.

To survive the collapse you have to remain invisible and that means not drawing attention to yourself. You don't want a visible garden, you just want an overgrown lawn that hides all the vegetables, so don't grow sweet corn or do any serious weeding. If you have apple trees or other fruit trees growing out the back it might be an idea to take all the visible fruit off so they don't attract attention. When we left our house in the suburbs, the neighbor asked if he could take some of the lemons. We were leaving so we said okay and he took the lot. I mean he cleaned out the tree. And that is what is going to happen if you have any fruit trees visible in your back yard. Except they wont ask.

NOW You Should Be Saving Seeds

Every time you buy any vegetable or fruit with seeds in it, save the seeds. Get into this habit now because seeds are the currency of the future. If you have plenty of seeds you can use them to barter with after things go from very, very bad to less bad. For example, when eating a watermelon save the seeds. Watermelons have lots of seeds so what do you do with them. To keep seeds you must dry them out so put them on some newspaper near a window in full sun until they are very dry. Then hang them up in the garage, garden shed or where ever in muslin bags. My mum used to put the seeds around the hot water cylinder to dry them out. Rats and mice love seeds so if you leave the seeds out over night you will probably find something has had lunch on your seeds. One night I left some seeds out in little trays on the window ledge and the next morning they had been eaten. So now when the sun goes down I hang up the seeds just to keep them away from anything that will eat them.

Saving seeds is a habit you should get into, it will pay off. We need seeds to survive the future when the supermarkets have no food. That will happen in your lifetime a lot sooner than you think. We are so dependent on oil and the cheap oil is running out. Also we are entwined with constant, cheap electricity and that is not going to last. The blackouts of the past are nothing compared to the blackouts of the future.

Another Good Habit Too Get Into

Something else you should be doing with seeds is throwing them around. This is another good habit to get into. When you go out take some seeds and just throw them around. Vacant lots are good places because I don't think any more vacant lots will be sold. The housing crisis has put a stop to any more houses being built.

So when you are walking past a vacant lot just walk in and throw some seeds around. In some vacant lots you will see gardens that have been growing for a while. These gardens are usually at the back and can't be seen from the road. So you are not the only one out there worried about the future. This way there will be vegetables growing in different places. Also start throwing seeds in places where your city council doesn't go. As the economic crisis deepens you will probably see the city start to lay off the park staff before the police and the fire fighters. After the park staff are laid off just start throwing seeds around the parks. Also along the edge of country roads and river banks. When you throw out climbing plants like cucumber, throw the seeds around trees so the plants have something to grow up. When eating apples, lemons and oranges and any fruit with seeds, save the seeds and throw them around. I threw some passion fruit seeds around a while back and now I can see them growing up the trees. Depending on your climate some fruit and vegetables are just not going to grow.

If you look around you there are no wild edible plants growing around the cities and towns. We have effectively wiped out all free growing vegetables and fruit trees. Modern farming methods and the city councils have effectively wiped out all self-seeding edible plants and trees. That is something that has to change. And it is up to you to change it. It doesn't take much to get climbing plants like cucumber and peas and beans growing up a few trees.

If you look around derelict buildings and old houses that have been deserted for years, there are no vegetables growing wild. They have all died out. So just to get some wild and free vegetables growing out there, it is up to you to throw some seeds around. After watching Life After People and The Colony, especially The Colony 2 in an area destroyed and left vacant by Hurricane Katrina, there were no vegetables growing wild or none that I could see. And that was a big area, so I thought there should have been, at least something growing wild. In Life After People when they take you to places that have been deserted for many years. I would have thought there should have been some wild vegetables or flowers growing in the backyards of the houses, but I didn't see any. So it looks like the vegetables and fruits we eat now are so adapted to living with people that they cannot survive without us. I've been throwing seeds around for years now and I'm amazed at what doesn't come up.

In some areas I've thrown lots of seeds around and nothing has come up. But every now and then I'll see a pumpkin or a watermelon growing and I know its working. So in reality I think wild natural gardens are just a dream. The plants are so adapted to live with mankind that they can't live without us. But I still throw seeds around especially in spring just to try and get some wild gardens seeded. I find that very surprising because when I lived in the tropics there were fruit and vegetables growing in lots of places. I wasn't living in a tropical paradise either, this was an overcrowded, over polluted city where the locals used to just throw the rubbish everywhere and that is probably why the plants grew.

Paw paws would grow anywhere, so if you were eating a paw paw and you dropped the seeds they would grow. Also mangoes were popping up all over the place. In some of the out of way places there were pumpkins and grapes growing wild. I think the reason these plants were allowed to grow is the people who looked after the gardens and the parks were farmers and they knew the plants so they wouldn't cut them down. I watched one guy with hedge clippers cutting a hedge and there was a little mango trees growing through the hedge and he cut around it. He didn't cut the mango tree. But then again in a park on the edge of a very polluted waterway there was this big mango tree with little mangoes growing all over it, and the park staff were throwing things at the tree to get the mangoes. Paw paw trees are different because they grow very fast and the paw paws were very soon out of reach. And the paw paws are hard to get down, but some guy would come along with a string bow sort of thing and get them down.

Now in a western city that just doesn't happen, so it is up to you to get the seeds out there. You should try and get hold of some heirloom seeds as these are possibly more hardy than the standard garden varieties. These are seeds your grandparents probably planted in their backyard gardens. First you should plant them in your garden and when you have plenty of seeds throw them around and see what comes up. When you grow your own vegetables let some vegetables like carrots, cabbage and most green vegetables go to seed so you have plenty of seeds. Now with the excess seeds go and throw them around your town, in vacant lots and in places where nobody goes. This will hopefully start a natural garden where the vegetables will reseed themselves and there will be plants growing there for years to come.

Now to recap: Get into the habit of saving seeds and throwing your spare seeds around in places where they have a chance to survive, so there will be food growing in many different places near your home. If you already live in a small country town this is a good hobby to get into. Even in the cities it is a good thing to do. Just remember mice and rats love seeds so keep a cat or two to keep the rats and mice under control. Keep an eye on all your little stashes of seeds to make sure the mice haven't been having lunch. You don't want to find that out when you need them. Another good idea is to have a rotation system where you start to distribute the older seeds out into the vacant lots when you have dried out new seeds. Try and get into the habit of saving nearly every seed you find in the fruit and vegetables you buy or grow. There will be a time when you will quite possibly not have enough seeds, especially if you are living off sprouts.

Chapter 6

Using Less

We live in a consumer society where we are bombarded with advertisements to use more, and to keep using more and more even if we don't need it. Now when things go from bad to very bad we will not be able to get those products we have been using all our lives. So just start using less, then use less and less until, if possible, you can do without. I first tried this with clothes washing soap. We have been brought up to believe we have to wash our clothes everyday, in the washing machine using incredible amounts of water and one and a half cups of soap powder to keep them clean. Anyway I thought I'd try not using so much soap and water to wash my clothes. I brought a couple of those big red buckets from the supermarket and now after work I throw my clothes into a bucket, fill it with water, no soap and just leave it. Sometimes I leave them overnight but that is mainly because I forget to hang them outside or in the garage if it is raining.

Usually I leave the clothes, towels and any other clothes that are not used very much in the bucket for a couple of hours or more then hang them outside. And I found they are still pretty clean. Now when my white shirts start to fade I'll throw them in a bucket will lots of soap and leave them to soak overnight. Next day I rinse them out and hang them up. The soapy water goes down the toilet and the rinse water goes in the big tank to water the garden. Next time the clothes start to fade I use the washing machine with soap. Soak them for about half a day in plenty of soap then start the washing machine up again. Now I wash all clothes and sheets, towels etc like this. Just soak them then hang them up. It is amazing how much we don't use the washing machine now.

Now with the modern water saving front loading washing machines it is probably better to use buckets, as you can get your clothes cleaner. The water saving machines just don't use enough water to get your clothes clean. That is what I think anyway. It would be better if you could put in a recycle water system to save water from the washing machine and that way you can still get your clothes clean and save water. For example the drain pipe from the washing machine, could go directly to the outside water tank that waters the garden. This way should use a biodegradable soap powder if the water is going on the garden. Everything you put on your vegetables ends up in your body. At the moment we don't put soapy water on the garden. Also we use buckets in the toilet, because with the water saving devices on the toilet there is not enough water to flush the toilet properly. When we are using buckets we are not wasting water, just recycling the used water.

Doing the dishes is a bit different. My wife has mastered the art of washing the plates and knives and forks without soap. She uses a sponge cloth and wipes everything clean. I put a big old saucepan in the sink and we wash the dishes in that. I use dish washing liquid, not the environmental friendly stuff as it doesn't do a very good job. This way we can recycle the soapy water down the toilet and the rinsing water goes to water the garden.

Another thing you can try is no soap when you shower. In the summer when I am covered in sweat I will not use soap every time I have a shower. That usually means a shower in the morning and then again after work. Now I don't use shampoo at all I just use some natural soap and I wash my hair with that. And it keeps it clean. Be very careful here because you can't smell how bad you smell. So if you are going to go without soap and just shower in water don't tell anybody. There are people out there who can smell anything as long as you tell them. Most people never get close enough to you to know what is going on so you should be okay. When I use soap I use a natural soap and I always wash my feet with soap. I always wash my hands with soap and water. In a pandemic washing your hands and not touching your face, including not touching your eyes, nose, ears and mouth, are a must to try and not gets the bugs. So don't stop washing your hands with soap. I'm just trying to use less and I picked on soap because we all seem to use too much of it.

Also another thing we are doing for a treat is putting Himalayan Salts in a bath and then throwing the water on the garden. Here we use no soap because we want the water to be soap free. There will be no more Himalayan Salts and soap when things start to fall to bits, so get used to not using them. Also now I don't use any sunscreen but I am very careful when I go out in the sun. Because we have the garden I spend a lot of time outside but I don't get sunburn. If I take my shirt off I time myself to an hour maximum in the sun as I know after that I will get burnt. Now I never buy sunscreen at all, sometimes some coconut oil but that is about it. Now I don't miss the sunscreen but it took a while to get back into being safe in the sun. Soap is the easiest everyday thing to go without, so start using less. But make sure you have enough soap to wash your hands. Things like toothpaste and toilet paper are pretty hard to go without so I keep using them. One place I am trying to keep away from is the supermarket, but it is difficult.

Chapter 7

Keeping Out Of The Supermarket

We as a species are too reliant on the supermarket. If the supermarket system ever breaks down we have severe problems. So I'm trying very hard to do without the supermarket but at present it is not possible. I rely on the supermarket for everything I need but that is getting less and less. Salt is the big thing. When the system breaks down where will I get salt from and we need salt. I've thought about evaporating salt water but as yet haven't tried it out. So even though I still rely on the supermarket I am thinking about how to live without it. I've turned the backyard into a garden so getting vegetables is not a problem. Also we get eggs from the chickens and we are thinking of getting some rabbits to see if that will work out. The most difficult to give up is processed food. We live off processed food and it tastes good. So you have to make a very conscious effort to stop buying processed food. Even after we had the garden producing more vegetables than we could eat, we still went to the supermarket.

It takes a long time to break the supermarket habit. Every time we went to the supermarket we just brought less and less. Starting with vegetables and now we buy what we need at the farmer's market. Now we buy very little processed food, mainly biscuits and luxury stuff like chocolates and red wine. When buying vegetables and fruit I try and buy ones with seeds. That is how we got our blueberry trees. Now with this talk of irradiating all food I don't know if the seeds will grow. Anyway I don't think food at the farmers market needs to be irradiated.

The hardest thing to change is breakfast and bread. Bread is a staple and is very difficult to do without. We have managed to cut right back on bread but we still buy the odd loaf now and then. When you stop eating bread you save on butter and many jars of jam. Glass jars and even plastic jars come in handy, so if I am buying something in a jar I try and buy the biggest jar. This way I have storage jars. We even bought a very big tin of biscuits so we could get the tin. If you can buy biscuits in tins, do so just for the tin. Even big plastic coca cola bottles can be used for storing dry food. So stock up on the plastic bottles. Get into the habit of not throwing things away. Because the things we throw away now, we will not be able to get very soon as they are made from oil. Breakfast is difficult but we managed to get over that by having eggs for breakfast. First it was eggs on toast now it is eggs without the bread. On the weekends I cook up a soup stew in the thermal cooking pot at night and that usually does breakfast and lunch. For breakfast I'll put some in a pan, heat it up then add some eggs. Pretty good, even the kid eats it.

When food shopping in the supermarket, look at tins and jars and see if the container is reuseable before buying it. When cheap oil goes containers could be a thing of the past as there is a oil content in nearly everything we buy. When I buy a bottle of water I always buy a clear bottle because you can use these to purify water, and they will come in handy when things go from less good to bad. Another big thing is milk we haven't got the cow yet. We are waiting for things to go from good to less good before we get into milking our own cow. So we get the milk from a friend who has too much milk. Barter system. The black and white cows produce a lot of milk. I'm looking at the little yellow brown cow, as they are not so big so they will take less to feed. When buying a cow, just remember when things go from bad to very bad someone might take your cow for food. Starving people don't think about all the milk you get from one cow, they will just be thinking about the cow as food. It is the same with the chickens. If you eat the chicken you will miss out on all the eggs. Try to tell that to the starving meandering mobs when they come calling. When you have animals running around your yard, you are at the mercy of horrible neighbors and bumbling bureaucrats. When the bird flu scare was on there was talk of destroying all backyard chickens. It was a worry but it never happened. We are lucky we don't have any pigs. The swine flu vaccine selling pandemic brought out the worst in people. Anyway the colony collapse syndrome wiped out our only hive of bees so there went the honey. We are still debating what to do with the empty hive. When the bees start living again we will get another hive. We had the last hive for years. All you need is one hive for all your honey needs.

It doesn't matter how many eggs you give your neighbors they will still complain about your noisy chickens, even though the roosters don't make any sound. It does help to be on friendly terms with your neighbors if you can. We know our neighbors, we talk to them but they are not into the future, so we can't really get them to start a garden or anything like that. They are just like the majority of the population, sleepwalking to very end. Neighbors can be a problem. There was an incidence that started when a neighbor complained about noisy chickens. In this case the losers are the neighbors as they will be looking for food when things come apart. It also looks like the law enforcement agencies could be a problem when things get tight. It will pay off to be under the radar. The more people who know you have food, the less secure you will be. The people who are featured on 'American Preppers' on National Geographic are just giving their advantage away. I try to remain anonymous and invisible. At least this way I might last a bit longer. Actually I'm quite worried about the future. Things around the world are not good. So a little bit of preparation will go a long way.

Chapter 8

You Will Need Water

Now the most important part of surviving the future is clean water, so where do you get clean water. Hydrogen Peroxide (H2O2) is a good start, as it will kill most of the bugs in water. Just a few drops in a bottle will do the trick. Hydrogen peroxide is a form of concentrated oxygen and most waterborne diseases do not like oxygen. That is why it is very good at purifying water. Also most of the bacteria in our stomach is anaerobic, that means they don't like oxygen either. So if you keep purifying your water with H2O2 you might change the composition of the bacteria in your stomach. Just keep that in mind. The cleanest hydrogen peroxide to use is food grade 35%. But be careful only a few drops in a bottle is all you need. And keep it away from your kids. In that concentration H2O2 is a poison and it will burn if you put it on your skin. It is a good idea to teach your kids about these things, just in case something happens to you.

Boiling the water is the best way but that is not always possible. You don't want people to know where you are and smoke will attract attention. Buy a magnifying glass and learn how to start a fire with it. Or you can go the "Survivorman" route and buy a flint and steel. Read the instructions and then go out and do it. It is no use buying the survival equipment unless you try it out, and survival equipment is what might save your life. One easy method is solar water. Use clear plastic bottles, full them about 90% with water, put the cap on and leave them in the sun to cook. And the ultraviolet rays will kill the bugs in the water. Glass bottles are just as good. The best place is on a tin roof or just on your concrete driveway. Somewhere that gets lot of sun. Just leave the bottles as long as you can in the sun. Roll them over a couple of times so the sun can shine on all the water. For this to work properly you need clear water so filter the water first, coffee filters are okay or just a squashed up T shirt will do after you have run out of filters. The sunlight should be able to shine right through the water bottle. Just remember to keep the bottles out of sight of passers-by as they will be thirsty too. Because you have to leave the bottles in the sun for hours on end you will need to keep them not visible from the road. Just keep that in mind.

Another easy method to purify water is with chlorine bleach. Again the water has to be clear so filter it or let it sit for a while and then scoop the clean water on the top into another container and add the bleach. You really need an eyedropper for this. You need about 8 drops per gallon of water or 2 drops for a quart of water. Leave it sit for about half an hour before drinking. If you can smell the bleach in the water it is good if not put another drop in. Only use regular bleach not the scented bleach. Bleach is good stuff so don't waste it. When you add bleach and hydrogen peroxide to water just remember you are also drinking it as well as the water. So only use it as an emergency and not for too long periods of time if possible.

I don't like to say this but I think water borne diseases will be your friend. They will thin out the population rather quickly. But the people you don't want around will most likely survive, as they will just take the bottled water from anyone by force. Also you will have to make sure your kids drink the bleach flavored water, and if your kids are like mine they wont want to do that. You will have to keep a sharp eye on your kids as I think most kids are going to be more difficult than they are now. To survive any breakdown in society whether it is a hurricane or a flood or another disaster, you will need to know how to make water safe to drink. So try out a few different methods, just to give you the confidence so you know you can do it.

Chapter 9

Basic Water Recycling

I have set up a very simple water recycling system just using those big red buckets you can buy from the supermarket. In the kitchen sink I have put an old big saucepan and I wash all the plates and knives and forks in the pot. I have a bucket by the toilet just to flush the toilet. All the soapy water goes in this bucket and is poured down the toilet. I don't use the flusher on the toilet as much as before mainly because it is a water saving toilet and it kept blocking up. All reasonable clean water goes into the big tank for watering the garden. I have a drip feed irrigation system in the garden. The big tank is a low big tank so I can pour the buckets into the big tank without too much effort. And this water is gravity fed through the garden. The big tank is only 6 inches higher than the garden and the tank is only 2 feet high so it is not too difficult to empty the buckets into. We put it on a concrete pad. I had to do this because the water restrictions wouldn't let us water the garden. And our garden is our food. Anyway to get more water to fill the garden tank, I changed the way I wash clothes. Instead of using the washing machine I just use buckets. When we all come home from work and school, we just throw all the used clothes and towels into a couple of buckets and fill the buckets with water, no soap. And we let then soak overnight then we hang them out on the clothesline the next morning. And that is it but I will add, when the clothes start to look shabby and the whites start to fade I throw them in the washing machine with lots of soap, and I mean lots of soap, double what they recommend. I let them soak overnight, run the washing machine and the soapy water goes into the toilet bucket. This brings the clothes back to life. Now some clothes can go two weeks, three weeks and even a month before they end up in the washing machine. I don't tell anybody at work that I just soak my clothes to wash them, because I don't know how they will react.

It is quite strange that when the water restrictions were in place. We weren't allowed to wash the car or water the garden or flush the toilet every time we used it. But nothing was said about the washing machine and that uses a lot of water. Anyway the system works. I now have buckets under the air conditioner pipes. I still use the air conditioner as the electricity is still going so we use it while we can. Anyway the kids wouldn't let me switch it off if I wanted to.

You need to have your own water supply and the easiest is to collect it from the roof of your house, unless you have a stream nice and handy. I've got one tank in the garage so it cannot be seen from the road and the other tank in the garden shed. I feel more secure with 2 tanks in case one breaks or springs a leak. And this way if the meandering mobs find one tank you still have the other one. You could also put in an underground water tank if you think you need one, and as long as you can completely hide it when necessary it should be safe. Some houses nowadays in desert areas have underground water storage tanks and when you visit the house you do not know there is a water tank under your feet.

Also I would keep the water tanks hidden because the council doesn't like them. When we had water restrictions the council never mentioned putting in water storage tanks. Even recycling water is not allowed so we have to use a rather covert system of carrying buckets around. City governments can be a problem when you are trying to survive the future. I wouldn't rely on them for help as they might try and stop your every move. I do this recycling thing not to save the world or to save on the water bill, but to give me an idea on how to save water when I need too. And I would add, anybody under 50 years old will see water problems in the very near future. In any collapse situation getting clean drinkable water will be a problem. So start now to recycle water as this way you are getting in some practice for when you need it. And you will realize the value of water. Right now we turn on the tap and the water comes out. But that situation will change very rapidly if there is any disruption in any of the systems we have come to rely on. Basic recycling water is something you should do so you already have a system in place when you need it. It is not about saving water it is about the future when the water stops running out of the tap. Having systems in place before a disaster is what will help you to survive the disaster. Clean drinkable water is one of the keys to survival so make sure you have a system in place that gives you clean drinkable water. I also have big bottles of water in the garage but these will have to be sterilized before you can drink them. They have been sitting there for a good number of years. Also I have covered them to keep the light away as light is not good on plastic.

Chapter 10

What If A Real Pandemic Hits

If a pandemic hits there are a few things you can do that will give you a better chance of survival. Most of the pandemics we have had so far are just media generated pandemics to sell vaccines. If a real pandemic hits I don't think there will be a vaccine. I think the news will downplay the severity of the illness. You'll just have to play this one by ear. I actually don't think a pandemic will take out the human race unless it is man made. Anyway I don't think nature will be so kind to us by throwing a pandemic at us. We have spent the last 100 odd years destroying nature. So I think nature will let us destroy ourselves slowly, by overpopulation, famine, resource depletion and wars. A pandemic is too easy. Anyway just in case I'm wrong and a pandemic heads your way, this is what you should do. You should keep your stomach acid levels very low, that means you need your body to be alkaline dominant. And the other thing you should also do is keep your blood sugar levels normal. It was shown that polio could not enter a body that had a normal blood sugar level.

How do you keep your blood sugar levels normal?

Now to keep your blood sugar levels normal is quite difficult, as nearly all processed food will lower your blood sugar levels. So will bread and all grains as well as root vegetables like potatoes and also fruit. That doesn't really leave you much else to eat except green vegetables and meat. Corn and tomatoes are also a no no. That is what the sprouts are for and to keep your acid levels down you shouldn't eat meat. If there is a polio type pandemic or any pandemic for that matter coming your way, just start eating green vegetables. That will help to normalize your blood sugar and acid levels. Also start eating raw garlic that has been crushed for about 15 minutes. Raw garlic will possibly be the best antibiotic around. I eat raw garlic everyday now and I haven't been really sick for a long time except I still manage to get a cold or the flu during the flu season. Garlic is very good for keeping intestinal worms and giardia under control. Giardia is an insidious little bug you get from water and eating undercooked meat mainly pork and you could end up with severe diarrhea for well over a month as well as a very upset stomach. The best way to eat garlic for upset stomach is to eat it first thing in the morning. Crush as many cloves of garlic as you want, I crush about six, wait 15 minutes then eat it. I cut the garlic into little bits so I can swallow it without chewing, this way you don't smell so bad. Now don't eat or drink anything for two hours to give it time to get to your small intestine to kill the beast. This beast is not easy to kill so keep eating garlic just to keep it under control. For other times I only eat it at dinner time as it will give you a serious case of bad breath. If your whole family eats it then for some reason you can't smell it on each other. I started eating raw garlic when I had a yeast problem and now I don't have a yeast problem. I would start growing garlic now, as you will need it. Also if you have too much you can just hang it up in the garage and it will dry out.

You will need some tinned and packaged food.

I am very skeptical about stocking up on processed food because of what it will do to your blood sugar levels. But you will need to have a store of dried food and tinned food. When the crisis hits it will be a good idea to divide up the packaged food put it in very strong plastic bags, like rubbish bags and hide it or bury it in different places. You can hide tins and dried food in the rafters under the roof, or even in the walls. I had to fix a water pipe so I cut of a big patch of plaster board to get to the pipe, and there were plenty of places to hide food. This way if your house is raided they will have less chance of finding all the food. And keep your sprouts out of sight, they are gold. To survive you must be invisible so don't throw you used food packets and tins out the front of your house. Bury them out the back.

A quick way to drop your acid levels.

Now to keep your acid levels low and your alkaline levels high you need good old Arm and Hammer Baking Soda or any baking soda for that matter. You want Baking Soda or sodium bicarbonate NOT baking powder. Baking soda is wonderful stuff. I mix it with H_2O_2 and water for toothpaste. To lower your alkaline levels in a hurry just put a teaspoon of baking soda in a cup of water and stir it all around until it is all dissolved. I usually leave it for about an hour before drinking. It is recommended to do this in the morning and also before you go to bed. During the 1918 Spanish Flu pandemic there were reports that families who drank the baking soda didn't get the flu. I don't think there have been any scientific studies done with baking soda so this could be an old wife's tale. But it is worth a try because there might not be too much else to do. And there seems to be a school of thought that keeps saying alkaline is more healthy than acid. That is why the alkaline diet is popular.

When I had stomach acid problems I used to use baking soda a lot and it makes you feel really good really fast, unless it is not dissolved properly. I think what happens when it is not dissolved is the baking soda dissolves in your stomach and froths up. Then you cannot burp and after you drink the baking soda drink the first thing you do is burp and then you feel better. So if you can't burp you will feel terrible so make sure it is dissolved. I usually left the solution of baking soda and water for about an hour before I drank it. This way it is usually all dissolved. You still see a few bits floating around in the bottom of the glass but they are okay. Now I use lifestyle changes so I don't use the baking soda as much as I used too. Baking soda is very hard to keep as it is in a cardboard box and baking soda absorbs moisture. So it goes hard very easy. I usually put it in a glass jar to keep it dry. It is amazing stuff so have plenty on hand just in case. I will give a warning here sometimes baking soda is a very good laxative but not always so just keep that is mind. I know one baking soda drink at night and one in the morning is a good laxative. Also to keep acid levels low you cannot eat meat, drink coffee or coca cola. Just stick to sprouts they'll keep your acid levels low. Lemons are good too. So to stay alive in the brave new word of the future you are going to need plenty of seeds for sprouts so stock up. Anyway after the world collapses coffee and coca cola will only be something we dream about.

Chapter 11

Food Storage

You will need to get into food storage sometime so start thinking about it and do some research. On the internet I am convinced some of the supposed experts are just plain wrong and should know better. I was reading an article the other day about what you should put in your food storage supplies and I agreed with hardly any off it. I'll come back to that later. When you build up your storage of food you must take into account that you might not have running water or electricity, so your fridge and stove might not be working. The most important item is for purifying water so stock up on unscented chlorine bleach; just get the pure chlorine bleach as this could save your life. To make sure it is always reasonable fresh use old bottles first. Just remember bleach will rot any clothing it touches. Don't wash your clothes in bleach because they will fall to bits while you are wearing them. You have been warned, but if you want to sterilize your food dishes, put a cap full of bleach in the washing water. This water can be reused as long as you can smell the bleach and the water is not to dirty. Another very important item that can also be used to purifier water is hydrogen peroxide. Get the 35% food grade $H2O2$, preferably in a dark colored bottled as sunlight will destroy $H2O2$ and you don't want that to happen. It is a poison and it burns so make sure your kids know that, and they also know how to use an eyedropper to measure out a few drops per bottle. H2O2 is a very good antiseptic so put it on cuts and scratches to kill the bugs. Stock up on eye droppers as they are very important.

I like Baking Soda but whether you get some or not is up to you. It makes good toothpaste when mixed with a little H2O2 and water. I use it for dropping acid levels in my stomach. If there is a flu pandemic you will need to have a very alkaline body and the easiest way to do that is a teaspoon of baking soda in a glass of water every two or three hours. That is why I like baking soda. A next must have is hand soap, not antibacterial soap. Find a brand that is unscented and reasonable natural and stock up on that. The reason I don't like antibacterial soap is there seems to be a backlash against it. Some doctors are blaming the increase in skin problems on the antibacterial soap. The story goes something like this: on our skin there is lots of bacteria and most of it is good, harmless bacteria but when you use antibacterial soap you kill all the good bacteria as well as the bad bacteria. Then again ordinary soap will kill all the bacteria anyway. But we use too many antibiotics and we are becoming resistant to the common diseases that our generation conquered. So I stay away from the antibacterial soap. You need soap. If there is a pandemic washing your hands could save your life. Do not touch your face during a pandemic. Wash your hands with soap and water before you wash your face. If there is very little water just use soap. Even now every time I come home the first thing I do after taking off my shoes is wash my hands with soap and water. Another good habit to get into.

I consider these four things very important but you also need vegetable seeds. Why stock up on food when you can grow it. You can grow seeds into sprouts for a quick meal but it could take about a week in summer. All you need is water and sunlight and you have food. So stock up on seeds and you will need about three or four sprouting trays. Seeds for bean sprouts can include alfalfa, wheat and barley seeds, all vegetables seeds and plenty of them in moisture proof and mouse proof packets. That is your food. If it looks like society is collapsing, start planting vegetable seeds in the back lawn. Don't dig it up just plant them in the grass. You don't want too many people to see your garden or them will be nothing left for you to eat. What you add to your food storage is up to you. You need salt, I like rock or sea salt in plastic waterproof packets. I would also start buying tinned fish and have plenty of tins in the cupboard. Tinned fish is very easy to eat so your kids are going to snack on it when you are not looking. You need the tinned fish because of the oil. To stay healthy we need oil and fish oil is better than a bottle of vegetable oil. I would consider buying cartons of tins of fish at the wholesaler if possible. Try and get the fish in oil, olive oil is best. If you look at the tinned fish it can come in brine or tomato sauce but I think the fish in oil is possible better for your health, because oil could be in short supply.

Now the size of the packets you buy depends on how many people are going to be eating it. You need waterproof containers for things like salt, milk powder and other dry goods. You do not want all your salt in one container put it in many small containers so if one gets wet you have many more. That goes for all your dry food products. Also you will want to be able to store your food in a number of different places. You do not want all your food in one place, in case of fire or the meandering mobs raid your house. When things go from bad to very bad, think about burying piles of food under your house where it is dry. In the back of the garage and in the wood shed under the wood except someone might try and steal your wood and find the food. In the rafters above your head is also a good place. Also in plastic rubbish bags buried in the garden with your vegetables growing on top to keep them hidden. Not really ideal as the water could rust the tins.

You want to be able to use up one pile of food before moving onto the next pile, so only have one pile visible at any one time. Therefore you must sort out the food into the different piles. Do not put all the tinned food in one pile and all the dry food in another because this way you'll have too many piles of food visible and you don't want that. So evenly distribute all your food into different hiding places. Just remember you don't need to do this until things go from bad to very bad very fast. After watching The Colony series if the colonists had hidden their food in different places then the meandering mobs wouldn't have been able to run away with so much of it. In The Colony 2 if they had hidden the food and medicine in many different places they would have been more secure. Where they were living they could not secure the building like they could in the First Colony series. After watching the first episode of the second series, that was their big mistake. If the food had been hidden and there were many places to hide it especially in the piles of rubbish, then they wouldn't have worried so much about the meandering mobs coming in and helping themselves. I would also have rubbed charcoal over the milk packets as they looked very new. When the three people had come in, if the food and goodies had been hidden, then they could have walked around and saw nothing. And you could have tried to make friends with them as opposed to keeping track of them.

I have never lived as a down and outer but in the British program "Filthy Rich and Homeless," they had very wealthy people living on the streets with homeless people. In that program the homeless people used to hide their stuff in little stashes scattered around their parts of the city. So that is something to keep in mind when you are living in an unsecured house. Keep your stuff well hidden so it is there when you come back.

Anyway back to food storage, when you buy new food for storage you should use up the old food already in your storage pile. So in your pantry or food cupboard have a rotating system like they do in the supermarket. Put all the new food at the back of pile or at the back of the line so you use the older food first. Now what do you put into your food storage. The golden rule is put in what you eat now as long as it is a balanced diet and is preserved. You are used to eating this food so keep eating it. But I would also throw in many packets of beef jerky because that will survive without the fridge and it goes well with sprouts. Tinned food is a must because you can eat tinned food without cooking it. But buy the better quality food because there is usually more food and less water in the tin. The tinned food I would stock up on is tinned fish whether tuna, salmon or sardines or whatever you like. You can eat this straight out of the tin and it is good for you. Also baked beans as opposed to spaghetti, as spaghetti has very little nutritional value. For sweet food I would throw in some tins of fruit salad, peaches and whatever fruit you like, possibly pineapple pieces. With tinned soup it you can't cook it, it won't taste very good so just think about that when you buy tinned soup. Will you and your kids eat tinned soup straight from the tin if you can't cook it. You will if you are hungry enough. I would buy dehydrated soup as it is easier to store than tinned soup.

Now the size tin you should buy should be the size tin you and your family can eat in one sitting. Because with the fridge down, you will not be able to save the leftovers. You must eat the whole tin, so that is the size tin you buy. We eat a lot of bread and food made from flour, now this will not be available when society comes unglued. So I recommend buying vacuum packed rice. Buy a little bag of rice just to get used to cooking it then buy a big bag for storage. I would like to have 3 big bags, use one and have two as back up. If you have diabetes, rice especially white rice, can be problematic. Rice is starch so it turns to sugar in your body therefore it will raise your blood sugar levels. Just keep that in mind when you stock up on rice. Any food that is vacuum packed should last longer as there is no oxygen in the packet. This way you are rotating packets of food.

Breakfast is the difficult meal to stock up on as most breakfasts are very fast food like add milk or water then eat and run. You know what breakfasts you and your kids like, so stock up on those. Your kids are not going to drink water that tastes like bleach so buy some powdered milk and mix that up. It might work but a lot of kids won't drink powdered milk. So hopefully your kids will eat bleach flavored breakfast cereal. I like oatmeal but that needs to be cooked but it possibly has more nutritional value than some breakfasts. Also stock up on treats like sweets or candies. I would buy the hard candies like barley sugars not the soft candies or chocolate. If you have got diabetes forget the candies, all processed food has sugar.

I would aim for as much extra food as you have space and money. Each week keep buying extra until you are confident you have enough food and seeds to keep you going. Keep all the food handy so you can use the older food first. Now start looking around your house and yard for possible hiding places. When things go from bad to very bad you should start hiding caches of food in many different places around your home and yard. If your home is raided then they will only find a small amount of food. And if your house catches fire you will still have some food outside but you might lose your water unless the tanks are underground. Another possibility is the meandering mobs might think your house in a good place to live and they might kick you out and shift in especially if there is water. So if you have food hidden outside you can sneak back and take it.

Now back to some of the stuff you find on the internet about what food to put into storage. Use your common sense about what to store. One article recommends you store 500 lbs of wheat and I assume that is wheat flour. I would recommend storing wheat seeds. If you never use wheat flour then don't store it. Anyway if the power is off you can't cook bread unless you have a fire oven. If you never use it don't buy it: that is the golden rule. The same article also recommends 100 pounds of sugar. Now that is ridiculous unless you have one hell of a sweet tooth. Anyway what can you do with sugar I never use sugar and if you never use sugar either don't buy it. Macaroni and macaroni cheese was also recommended along with 75 cans of soup. Buying cans of soup is ridiculous. It is better to buy dehydrated soup mixes and boil them up with water. And there are more nutritional types of dried food than macaroni and macaroni cheese. Use your common sense when buying food for your food storage.

When in the supermarket look at what is available and buy a few. Like a bag of vacuum packed rice. That should last a long time but you need to be able to boil water to cook the rice. That is where your thermal cooker will come in handy so have a practice run boiling rice in the thermal cooker. There is a lot of food available in a supermarket so look around. Look at containers and see if you can reuse them. Containers will be like gold after things go from bad to very bad. So save all the big plastic coke bottles as they make very good storage containers.

Now finding water could be a problem but we'll get into that later. One thing I do agree with is buying multivitamins. Now when you buy any medicine or supplements buy the best quality and that will mean buying expensive brands. I never buy the cheap brands of vitamins because they are useless and they do not last a long time. I would recommend buying Spirulina, as it is a super food and it contains lots of natural vitamins and minerals. If you live in a tropical area see if you can get some spirulina culture and grow your own. Check it out on the internet. It seems quite easy to grow but you need heat and it doesn't grow in cold climates.

Another recommendation I don't agree with is buying aspirin as I think aspirin are useless and I never take them now, so I am definitely not going to start when the world starts to collapse. I do recommend stocking up on antibiotics as they will be gold. I'm quite lucky, well really I'm not, I have an impacted wisdom tooth and the gum under the tooth keeps getting infected so the dentist put me on antibiotics. The antibiotics clear it up but it always comes back. I was a bit worried about taking antibiotics all the time so I checked out the internet. And there I found the baking soda, hydrogen peroxide with water mixture. So I started using that and now I save the antibiotics. But there is a warning you can't use the mixture all the time because your teeth will start to tingle. When I first started using the mixture I used it all the time and I got the tingling, so now I only use it when I have the infection. I'm a bit worried about what will happen after the world collapses and there is no more hydrogen peroxide or antibiotics. They say eating raw garlic might stop the infection. I hope anyway because when you have an infection and no antibiotics you could be in serious problems. That is why I like baking soda and H2O2 so much.

Chapter 12

Living Without The Fridge

Living without the fridge is a new experience. Modern man hasn't lived without a fridge for the last 40 to 50 years, so we are in for a big shock. To find out what life was like without the fridge you will have to talk to somebody over 50 years old. They would have been brought up without a fridge. Anyway we will have to live without the fridge after the electricity goes off and doesn't come back on again. To survive without a fridge you will have to rearrange your whole life. And that will start in the garden. When you start planting your garden, plant in an as you eat rotation system. That means only plant what you think you can eat at one time. I plant between one and two meters every weekend. I'm trying to get a system where I have enough food to eat straight from the garden. Very difficult but I'm working on it. And any fresh vegetables that are surplus I dice them up and try drying them. I haven't started preserving food in jars yet but that is on the agenda. I plant by seeds and if they don't come up or the slugs and snails get them I just plant another seed in the vacant spot. For example I'll plant just 4 cabbages, 10 carrots and 1 cucumber, and next time 1 zucchini, because they produce a lot of vegetables on one plant and just one tomato seed or plant at a time. I try not to plant too many seeds at once. One pea plant and one bean plant each time. This way you have a rotation of vegetables ready to eat. I don't plant in rows any more, everything is just scattered around growing through the grass.

Start with a practice run, throw some seeds around and see what happens. Just start with a meter square in the corner of the lawn and as you get better at growing vegetables add another meter. Don't start by digging up the lawn as that will put you off growing your own vegetables before you have any to eat. Just start small because you can always get bigger. And if society collapses when the power goes off just plant your garden like this. Do not plant too many seeds at once. Because you might have to move and you will need seeds to start your garden when you find a place to settle down. Also if you are living of sprouts while your garden is growing go easy on the seeds. You don't want to waste any. And it will take well over a month to get any food from your garden. Radishes are a very fast growing vegetable, so plant them first. Anyway you always end up with more food than you can eat at certain times and at other times like winter there is very little food just kale and some winter hardy vegetables.

So to start living without the fridge you need a rotation of food available when you need it. Also you can only cook what you can eat. There is no more putting the leftovers in the fridge for tomorrow sort of thing. For the meat side of things this is where chickens and rabbits come in. One family can eat one rabbit or one chicken with very little left over at one time. You can make a soup in the thermal hot pot and leave it cook slowly all night then eat it all the next day. The fridge has made life very easy for us as it extends the shelf life of food very easily. Put vegetables in the fridge and they last a long time. Tomatoes will last a long time in the fridge but hanging up in a cheesecloth cupboard in a breeze they might last a couple of days longer than sitting on the window ledge. Eggs are usually okay out of a fridge but milk isn't so if you have a cow or a goat you'll be drinking the milk straight from the cow. If you get a cow get a small yellow jersey cow as they don't make as much milk as a big black and white cow.

To live without a fridge you just have to think short term. Like day to day to do with meals, so there are no leftovers. You'll be living from the garden to the table with no fridge in the middle. In the documentary "The Colony 2" they made the mistake of cooking up too much food after the trader came in on his boat. And they also made a wrong choice. They didn't know what to do with the left over food. They had a choice of leaving it out so anyone could help themselves, or trying to store it. And they chose to store it and it went off and had to be thrown away. The fridge mentality lives on. So stick to a schedule of cooking up as much as you can eat and eating all the leftovers.

Chapter 13

Easy Vegetable Storage

You have a vegetable garden and lots of vegetables so how do you store them. A lot of roots, tubers and bulb vegetables can stay in the ground like beets, carrots, parsnips, rutabagas, and turnips until you need them. Just cover with a mulch of straw or hay about 1 to 2 feet thick - that is a lot of straw. But if your area is very wet or very cold the vegetables can be damaged. And if the ground freezes you can have problems getting the vegetables out of the ground. If you have no straw or hay I just put all the green material from the garden that I don't eat back on the garden. I don't do compost anymore, I use a natural farming method. This is a good mulch I rake up leaves from the local park and along the roads to use as mulch. Mulch is something I usually run out of so I collect the leaves. They are the easiest to get.

Now potatoes don't do too well in the ground so they need to be stored in a root cellar. Which is a cool, dry dark place like an old cupboard or wardrobe in the garage or basement. Or just under your house if you can get under it and it is dry. Here you have to be careful about mice and rats, get a cat. The best vegetables for a root cellar are beets, carrots, parsnips, potatoes, pumpkins, rutabagas (swedes), turnips and winter squash. If you live near a sandy beach you are very lucky as you have plenty of sand and vegetables store well in sand. With old wooden boxes or plastic buckets start with sand and alternate layers of vegetables and sand until you fill up the box or bucket. When you are doing this make sure the boxes or buckets are where they will not be moved, as they are quite heavy. Root crops can be stored this way. If you do not live near a beach you can use straw instead of sand.

Garlic is a must when the world ends as it has incredible health benefits. The Roman army marched on garlic. So grow it and store it. With garlic and onions cut the tops and or roots off about half an inch away from the bulb. Dry in the sun for a week to three weeks then hang up in mesh bags or net bags in the garage in a windy place. Don't put too many bulbs in a bag. If they start to sprout, eat them. You must store garlic, as it will probably be the only antibiotic available. But garlic does not last much over a year. You might find when you go to get some garlic from your little bag hanging up in the garage that all the cloves have turned to dust. Try not to leave it to long, use it up it is good stuff. With pumpkins and squash put in a dry place and move occasionally. Tomatoes pick green and ripen slowly. In the middle of summer when there is a lot of sun dice or slice vegetables and sun dry them. Stock up on mesh bags, net bags and cheese cloth and hang up in the garage to stay dry. Storing vegetables is not that difficult. With a bit of extra care and covering at the right time you don't need a fridge. Anyway after the electricity goes off your fridge will be go off with it. Now is the time to practice vegetable storage without the fridge or freezer and without preserving them. If your garden has a good crop just try out different storage methods to see what works best for you. Now, before your safe suburbia comes apart, is the time to have a go at what you need to know before the electricity goes off.

Chapter 14

Use The Sun

The sun has had a pretty bad rap lately but when our modern life comes to an abrupt end, we are going to be living in the sun again. And it will not be all that bad. Ultra violet rays from the sun are actually very good for us. Leaving clear plastic or glass water bottles in the sun for over 4 hours, rolling occasionally will actually purify the water. The bottles must be in the sun as long as possible. The water needs to be filtered so it is pretty clear before you put it in the bottles. Basically the sun has to be able shine right through the bottle. In India now there are ultra violet light water sterilization units in small villagers. They purify the water for the whole village and they are very cheap to run and install. If there is a pandemic leave everything in the sun to kill the bugs. Anything you buy just leave it in the sun, turning occasionally so the sun's rays get on all the surfaces to kill any bacteria or viruses on the surface of the tins. Like if you buy food at the supermarket during a pandemic before you take it inside leave it in the sun. The suns rays seem to be able to kill bacteria and viruses but not all will be killed. So to play it safe and keep washing your hands and do not touch your face.

If you can't wash your clothes just hang them out in the sun to air and this should get rid of most of the bugs. I don't know if staying in the sun will help you not get the pandemic, but lying in the sun in the middle of the day might help. Half an hour front and half an hour back should kill the bugs on your body and clothes. I must stress do not get sunburn as this is very bad for your skin, possibly causes cancer and it will leave you wide open for diseases to get into your body through your burnt skin. Honey is very good for burns, the ancient Egyptians were using it 5000 years ago so why not use honey if you get sunburn. If you can get a beehive then you will have all the honey you will need. If you have an outside clothesline use it. Hang your blankets and sheets and spare clothes up during the day to catch the rays and hopefully to kill the bugs. Also you can use the clothesline to hang up food to be dried, like meat.

The latest from the alternative health people is the sun will help you not get the flu. They say the sun causes your body to make Vitamin D and Vitamin D stops the flu. But they do stress do not get sunburn. They recommend 20 minutes to half an hour most days at lunch time will give you all the Vitamin D you need to stop the flu. I don't know how accurate that information is, as I spend a lot of time in the sun when I'm in the garden and I still managed to get a massive dose of the flu this year. I used hydrogen peroxide in my ears and that seemed to help. I just put a few drops of H2O2 in one ear and lay down on my side for about half an hour then changed sides. I also tried out the baking soda mix to drop my acid levels to see if that would stop the flu. If there is a serious pandemic use baking soda to keep your body very alkaline, as that might stop you from dying from the flu.

When society breaks down there will be no more medicine or doctors so start to pick up on what the natural health community is saying, it might save your life. I think modern medicine is a thing of the past. We'll be going back to the Middle Ages with our medical knowledge. And the sad thing is the diseases modern medicine has conquered will return. Last time I got the flu I didn't go to the doctor or buy any medicine. I just used hydrogen peroxide in my ears and a half a teaspoon of baking soda in a glass of water, morning and evening. I just wanted to see what would happen. Well I got a big shock. The flu lasted about three weeks and I just couldn't throw it off. It was quite bad. I didn't really know what to try, so things are not going to be very good after society comes apart. Expect it.

Chapter 15

Have A Practice Run Drying Food

When the electricity goes off your fridge is going to go dead. Usually electricity blackouts happen in the summer, except for the ice storm that destroyed Montreal. But in the middle of a Montreal winter your fridge shutting down is the least of your worries. Modern man has lived out of a fridge for as long as I can remember so living without one is a big change. The blackouts of the past are going to return. That is a given, the only thing we don't know is when. So to prepare for the fridge shutting down you should have a few practice runs drying food. Drying vegetables is no problem. You just need to chop them up into dryable sizes leave them out in the sun, turn them over, bring them in at night and then put them back out the next day. In good sun 2 to 3 days should be okay. I usually throw a bit of sea salt on them before I put them in the sun, just to add some flavor. After they are dry, hang them up in muslin cloth bags so the air can get through them. It is a good idea to shake them up occasionally so the outside pieces are not always on the outside.

Practice with different sizes when you cut up the vegetables just to see what is best. Also have a go with fruits like apples, watermelon and pears. When cutting up moisture laden fruit and vegetables don't cut them too small or they will dry away to nothing. With tomatoes just cut them up into quarters. You are drying out the fruit and vegetables for survival food because the fridge is no longer going. So with meat you are making your own beef jerky. Again practice, slice the meat into long slices about half an inch thick. I don't cut the fat off but some recommend it because it takes longer to dry. Now I thread the slices onto a nylon fish line and hang up outside on the clothesline. This way the cats can't get it but birds and flies can. As long as the meat starts to dry fast you won't have too many problems with flies. Flies like wet meat. Wind and sun is what you want. You can also put the slices of meat in baking trays with muslin cloth covering them to keep out the flies. If you put the trays outside on the concrete they should dry out pretty fast. It is recommended to put the trays on chairs or stools, so the wind can blow around the trays. The wind is very good at drying.

I'm just mentioning practice runs with drying food so you know what you are doing when you need to do it. Dried food is not always safe to eat. The dried food you buy has preservatives on it so it will keep. Also we usually keep dried food in the fridge. So what do you do when you have no fridge? Cook all the dried food if you can. I make a soup with the dried vegetables and jerky and a bit of sea salt. I use a thermal cooking pot because it saves energy. I just boil the soup up for about 10 minutes then I put the soup in the thermal cooking pot and leave it for about three or four hours. Before you cook any dried food just smell it to make sure it is alright to eat. In the old west the Indians used to make buffalo jerky. They would make the jerky in the autumn then when winter set in the jerky would freeze outside. That is why they could live off it. So if you don't live in a cold climate in winter cook the dried food.

In The Colony 2 they made a smoke house out of plywood and tried smoking some fish. Here they could have made a tripod and hung up a supermarket trolley or something like that. Then put the fish in the trolley and just hung it up over the fire they used to boil water. It would have dried out. It just shows if you can do a practice run then you have a better understanding of what you are doing. They should have left the fish out in the air to dry more but they wrapped it up and it got fly blown and there were a few maggots crawling over it. Then they threw it away, and a couple of other guys picked it up and started eating it. At least they tried but they didn't know what they were doing. So after you have had a few practice runs drying food then you won't make those mistakes. If you have caught some fish while you are out camping, hang them out in the sun and wind to dry and see what happens. Or set up a tripod high over the fire and try drying them out that way.

In the tropics it seems to be quite common to dry out meat, fish and vegetables in the autumn. Where I was living in Asia you would always see fish and meat hanging of clothes coat hangers in the direct sunlight and in the little wind there was. Just walking home from the bus stop I would meat hanging in lots of places. Also in the supermarket you could buy dried meat and dried fish. It was very popular and tasty. I would never eat it raw I always cooked it. Also you would see vegetables drying on the hot concrete, once when I was walking by the polluted river there vegetables just lying on newspaper drying in the sun.

And that is a habit you have to get into. To start just dice some carrots and put them in the sun to see what happens. Then after they are dried hang them up in muslin bags to see how long they last before they go bad. They should last a long time. Then after you have got into the habit of drying vegetables try drying meat. If you are out camping you can try smoking it. But if you are still in suburbia just hang the meat in the sunlight and wind and see what happens. You need to try out these new methods so you know what you are doing when you need to do it. Then if you are already drying vegetables and meat when disaster strikes you just need to continue.

Chapter 16

Simple Sanitation Methods

When society starts to go from not good to bad and the electricity goes off. There is a chance it will not come back on again for a while then it is time to start preparing your home. If you do not have a water tank and even if you do, fill the bath and all buckets with water just in case. If the power goes off the water will soon run out. And you need water. If the power comes back on again you can put the water in the tank in the garden. But it is better to be safe than sorry. You do not want to run out of water. Water is life and don't tell your neighbors you have water. If you are on good terms with your neighbors suggest storing water. We have a small wooden bath we can move around so we can hide that when it is full of water. Now the toilet, if the water goes off stop using the toilet as that is a waste of water. If society looks like it is breaking down and you live in a house with a yard, dig a hole out the back and put up a simple teepee tent over it and use that. Stick it in the corner somewhere. If you live in a flat with no backyard put a plastic bag inside the toilet bowl so the edges of the bag hang outside around the bowl. And use that for solids. For liquids just use an old pot you can tip down the balcony drain. With the toilet either put a flat board over the toilet to keep the flies out or better still tie the bag shut after use. Then you can open it when you want to use it. When it is full or needs to be emptied just pull the bag out and put another one in. Put the full bag outside and take it away at night. You don't want flies getting anywhere near this bag. Just remember to set up a place to wash your hands. Put a cap full of bleach in a bucket and keep using that bucket. When the bleach smell goes away put some more bleach in and use the same water unless you have plenty of water. You must try and stay healthy. Eat raw crushed garlic everyday.

Don't use bleach on your body because it is not good. The skin on your hands and feet is tougher than the skin on your body. And bleach will kill all the bacteria on your body, the good and the bad bacteria. If you want to have a wash just use a bucket of ordinary water and a cloth and just wipe yourself down. When you have plenty of water and society looks safer then you can start to use soap. Go easy on the soap as you can't buy anymore. Look after your health, try and keep your hands away from your face. Do not touch your eyes, mouth, nose or ears if possible. If you get sick, the flu or something like that, put some 3 or 5% hydrogen peroxide solution in your ears and leave for as long as you can. Lie on your side and the solution bubbles and hisses away, then after half an hour change sides. Just remember doctors will be hard to find and medicine will be even harder to find. You are on your own. It might be a good idea to buy a book on natural medicine just in case.

Chapter 17

How To Stay Invisible?

After society comes unglued there will be groups of people who want to take what you have. Most people in society are decent but they will do bad things to survive. Groups of children will probably be very dangerous. They are not supervised and they do not know the line between good and bad. And they might start to act out what they see on TV. So keep away from groups of children because you do not want to hurt them but they don't care what they do to you. I'm very careful about groups of children. Twice in developing countries I was basically mobbed by kids and there was nothing I could do except put my hands over my pockets and run. There were little hands going everywhere, taking everything they could grab. So I ran and hopped they didn't trip me up or anything like that. Another guy I met said he had just walked out of the supermarket and the kids mobbed him and took all his groceries. These kids just don't care so if you see groups of kids just keep out of sight.

You do not want to attract attention so no lights or candles at night. If society degrades completely make your house look like it has been looted by throwing old clothes and useless stuff out the front. You could even smash the windows at the front of the house and live out the back. It depends on how bad things are in the area you live in. If you have solar panels on the roof take them off because they attract attention. You do not want people visiting you to take them because they will see what else you have. If you want to recharge your batteries just lay the panels on the lawn out the back to catch the rays. Then bring them in at night. Don't let anybody know you have electricity all they might try and take it.

It is possible that most groups will have some guns but you can safely work on the assumption that they don't want to use them. There will be some full-time nutters out there and they are the people you should be very wary of. But full time nutters should stand out in the crowd. Treat everyone with caution but you will need to talk to people. Not everyone will be a full-time nutter, there will still be a lot of good people out there. But even good people will do desperate things to survive. Full-time nutters are usually predictable and you can see them coming. So you have time to get out of their road or to stay out of sight or whatever. But there are going to be a lot of good people out there, who are desperate. Parents who haven't eaten for days with very hungry kids and parents with very sick kids, and they don't know what is going on. These desperate people will be everywhere, and desperate people will do desperate things on the spur of the moment. And these are the people who will cause problems. They are usually very reasonable people but now we are in very unusual times, so you don't know what they are going to do. Also they have brains and you will encounter intelligent desperate people who can think through situations. So that is why you have to be invisible.

Don't give anybody the impression you have food and water. Keep everything well out of sight. When you go out wear the dirtiest clothes you have and have a bag so it looks like you are scavenging, and carry a club or something for a weapon. Don't carry anything on you like clean water or tinned food. Just carry a dirty bottle of dirty water and don't look too healthy. If anyone finds a clean bottle of water on you, you are in trouble and so is your home. When you come home make sure you are not followed and climb over the back fence to get into your house. Don't use the front door. If the meandering mobs of desperate people think you have something you will become a target. And you don't want that. If you carry a gun make sure it is hidden as some people might knock you down to get your gun. If you end up in a situation where the meandering mobs are coming for you then you might have to show your gun. I work on the assumption that most people will back away when guns come out unless they are full time nutters. Most people do not want to get hurt or killed so they might back away. And you should do the same.

Now what do you do when people come knocking on your door and that will happen. This situation is very difficult because if you give them anything they will most likely come back and worst they could sell you out. Now that will happen. They could get a mob together and come back to raid your house. So if you are pretty well fortified you can afford to be a bit charitable, but if you live in an ordinary house in suburbia that is basically unprotected you cannot let anybody know what you have. If people come knocking you can invite them in for a chat so they can see you have nothing. Make sure you have nothing visible. Most people will be after food and water so hide your food and bleach in different places in or around your home. Bury some in the garden out back as well as some under the house and more hidden in the garage.

They will raid your garden when you are asleep so expect it. If you have any fruit trees that are visible take all the fruit off so the meandering mobs don't meander out back to take the fruit and anything else that they like. If you and your neighbors can gang up together then things will possibly be safer. You might have to help plant a garden or two just so your neighbors have some food then they wont take yours. Another situation that will pop up is some people will want to join your little group. I work on the assumption "the more the merrier" because the more people in your group the safer you will be. But you have to feed them and give them water, so you have to decide are they going to help you or hinder you. Just after society starts to fall to bits you could round up your friends and relatives and bring them all together at your place. If people want to join your little group then that is up to you. You have to decide if they are going to be safe. That is another reason why you should have your food and bleach stashes hidden in different places around your home. If the people turn against you and kick you out then you can sneak back and recover some of your hidden supplies.

Another thing you have to be careful of is packs of dogs. Dogs will band together and they will be looking for food. When Hurricane Katrina hit New Orleans there were stories of packs of dogs worrying people. The dogs were looking for something to eat. And the same thing will happen after society collapses. Normally if you are confronted by an aggressive dog you go into the submissive stance. That is, look down and keep your hands in front of you. Never look a dog in the eye and never try to outrun a dog because you can't. But if these dogs are after you as food, things could be very different. I don't know the difference between an aggressive dog and a hungry dog. If you are in a situation with a pack of dogs try and get into a car, climb a tree or just get to a safe place but never run. If you run a dog will chase you and then you are at a disadvantage because your back is to the dog. All big aggressive dogs can outrun you and if they bite your leg and you go down you are finished. When you get knocked down by a dog you should go into the "like a log" position. That is you curl up into a tight ball with your knees up against your stomach. And your face on your knees with your hands over your ears and arms guarding your neck. That is what you are supposed to do now in a normal society and somebody will help you. But things could be very different very soon so I would keep out of the road of any dogs, just in case. If you can get your back against a wall you'll be in a better position. Just be very careful if you see dogs. Carry a big heavy stick or club so you can hit the dog on the head. This won't do any damage as dogs have a very hard head, but it might give you some time but not much. Dogs will be a problem. Also if you own a dog then be careful as hungry people will be looking at your dog as food. Keep your dogs out of sight. I would just use them for protection around your home. I wouldn't go walking the dog anymore. After society breaks down dogs and cats will be the first to be eaten, then onto the rats and mice. If you have chickens you will be a target because people can hear them in the morning, so get your roosters fixed so they are quiet. Rabbits are better because they are quite but there are no eggs.

Chapter 18

Guns And Groups

I'm not really into guns but I have friends and relatives who are and that is fine with me. I can shoot if I have to and I was actually quite a good shot when I was younger, but now I leave that for the younger generation.You can safely assume most people will have guns so you do need one or two. I'm no expert but my friend who goes to the gun club is and he makes his own bullets. He has the molds and the detonators and he puts it all together. In a world that is collapsing making your own bullets is a plus. So before you buy a gun make sure you can get the molds and detonators so you can make the bullets. Bullets are going to become very hard to find just a few days into a collapse scenario. Either be prepared and able to make your own or start stocking up because you are going to need them. Anyway you can trade bullets but that will leave you wide open to anyone who wants to steal your molds. Just be careful with guns because once you are shot you are finished. Modern medicine is a thing of the past. First you will be using guns for protection, but if you are walking around by yourself keep your guns out of sight. You don't want to attract attention.

Now before the world collapses it might be an idea to join a few groups to learn a few skills. I think the first thing you should learn is self defense. There are self defense classes in most gyms so I would join one as it could save your life. As my instructor said if you know just 10% more than your opponent you have a chance. And that is all you need, a chance and that could make a difference. So I put self defense on the top of my list of things to learn, just for the confidence boost. Now I'm trying to get my kids to learn self defense and that is a big task.

Another thing you should know is how to swim so if you don't know how to swim, learn because it could save your life. Also do survival training as that helps. There they threw us in the pool to see how long we could stay afloat in the water. I didn't last very long but I'm getting better. At least I know how just in case I need too. The survival training is good because you are out in the forest and you do learn things that will come in handy. It is another one of those just in case things. Now we go camping and hiking in the wilds and it is a lot of fun so join a camping club and have some fun. We are now looking at joining a riding club so we can try out riding a horse. That could be a lot of fun too.

Join a gun club to learn how to shoot and keep safe around guns. After collapse sets in guns are going to be a part of your life so start early then you will be one step ahead of most people. Learn skills so you have an understanding of what you can do and what you need to learn. Also you might meet like minded people that are learning new skills just in case because they think the world is going to collapse. And these are the people you could put into your little band of survivors. And you might see places you could run too when things go from bad to very bad. Keep your eyes open for possible retreats you can get to if you need to. This way you can tell your family we will meet here if we get separated.

Another very important skill you should try out is fishing. Just to see how difficult it is to catch a fish. I must admit it is not easy so get in some practice. Fishing is becoming more and more popular lately. Possibly because the unemployment rate is going up and it gives the people something to do. When I go down to cities on the coast I see more and more people fishing but I have never seen anybody catch anything. Where I live on a river I see many people catching fish and there are more and more giving it a go. Also you could buy a few spring loaded rat-traps and see if you can catch any big rats. All cities have rat problems so it should be a good exercise in getting your own food. Whether you eat them or not is up to you. It is just a practice run.

A very important skill you should look into is basic medicine where there is no doctor. A basic first aid manual should teach you the basics but when things go from bad to very bad there will be no doctors. So the knowledge you have will keep your little group alive. Most of the adults in your group should learn basic and not so basic first aid. It could save your life. You could start off by doing a first aid course and moving up from there. The most important knowledge could very well be natural antibiotics as antibiotics would be like gold. So you need to live without them. And so far I have found nothing that will take the place of antibiotics. So we are in for a very rude awakening when we run out of antibiotics. For the past 60 odd years we have been very lucky with antibiotics and vaccinations. But those days will end very fast as society starts to degrade into chaos. Also we are using antibiotics in animal feed so we are slowly but surely breeding resistance. And we might see, in the very near future, an antibiotic resistant super bug and then we will have serious problems. We are not prepared for a world where antibiotics don't work.

Knowledge has to be spread around. If you have all your information on your hard drive and the power goes off then it is useless. So buy books and keep them in a safe place. Just remember medical books and survival books will be like gold so keep them hidden. And read them and do some of the things mentioned like starting a fire without matches.

Chapter 19

Bring Change on Slowly

If you want to bring in these new ideas to your family they will probably think you have gone mad, at least mine did. What I did was start talking about things like the world running out of oil and climate change and any natural disaster that had befallen the world. Then I started talking about doing things about it. All the while, stocking up on food and trying to turn the backyard into a garden. Mind you my daughter thought I was nuts and still does but she realizes something could happen. Bringing in the simple water recycling system was very easy. Where we live we had water restrictions because of the drought. And once I had the water system in place it stayed. And that was the same with washing the clothes. Putting in the little water tank for the garden helped keep the buckets in use. We still use buckets everyday. Habits are hard to get into but once they have been set up they are very hard to break. And breaking the habit of the washing machine is quite difficult. But we managed and now we hardly use the washing machine at all but it is there when we need it. If you buy good quality clothes they seem to survive quite well just being rinsed in a bucket to get the sweat off. Now it seems ridiculous to load up the washing machine with clean clothes. Your clothes are not going to get dirty just wearing them one day in an office.

After talking about the world running out of oil, it turned out that my daughter's best friend actually knew about it. And her father had already brought a block of land and one of the relatives was living there and had turned it into a sort of makeshift domestic animal zoo. So when you change you will meet people that think the same way. But don't expect your neighbors to start planting a garden just because you do. I'm actually quite lucky as my sister is into urban survivalism and she has the chickens and the ducks and had the bees before the colony collapse syndrome wiped them out. We'll get the bees back sometime they were good. They live in the middle of suburbia and they are not the only ones with chickens. In the morning you can hear rooster's crowing in many directions.

Also you'll be amazed at how many people just don't know the world is running out of nearly everything. And they haven't a clue what to do if the supermarket closed down. "The technology will save us" crowd is in for a big shock. If the electricity goes off a lot of people wouldn't know what to do. They'll do what they have always done, waited for it to come back on again. But one day it will not come on again. So the big thing is just do something to get started. I'm not talking about doing without. Still use the internet, the TV and everything that runs on electricity. And the car, but buy a bicycle just in case. We are talking about being prepared, buy some sprouts and see how long they take to grow so you know. But do it more than once, get into the habit of growing and using sprouts, see how long they take to grow in spring, autumn and winter, so you know. Find the best place to put the trays so they grow the best. Just remember to bring them in at night so the slugs and snails don't eat too many of them. When you have too many vegetables try drying them to see how to do it and then how to cook them. Buy a thermal cooking pot and use it so you know what to do when you have to. Learn how to start a fire with a flint and steel and then with a magnifying glass. Show your kids and wife how to do it just in case something happens to you. Surviving the future is a family affair, so all work together. Just you learning the new skills is not a good idea. Everybody needs to be able to survive using the basics but you should all specialize in one area. Like medicine, guns, gardening or looking after the bees.

Chapter 20

If You Have To Move

You must have an exit plan if things go from bad to very, very bad very quickly. Now you have a stockpile of food and seeds and things you need to survive the future so how do you move it. You can basically guarantee cars are finished as there is no gas and it would not be safe to use a car. You would be a target and you don't want that. Or you could do what the first colonist in The Colony did and build a truck, but I don't think many people could do that. So what do you do when you are surrounded by meandering mobs and it is not safe to go anywhere but you have decided to move and you want to move out of the city.

The first thing I would do is find a safe house two or three hours away from where you are now in the direction you want to go. And that usually means into the countryside where there is water and places to grow things and keep animals. Now you will need to split up your group. Send someone to live in the safe house to see if it is really safe and start moving all your possessions slowly between the two houses. But don't move too much at once in case the mobs stop you and take what you have. Even before you have completely moved from one house to the next you can set up your third safe house and even a fourth and this way you have stuff stashed in many different places. You do not want all your eggs in one basket. This way you can move out of the city and into the countryside and hopefully have all your stuff with you. Moving will take time and planning, there will be no more of this jump in the car and go. It could take you well over a year to get settled again. Make sure you are settled for the winter so keep the seasons in mind. Also you can set up trays of sprouts in each different house so you have something to eat.

As the cities turn to chaos rats will be a problem and I think there could be swarms of rats in parts of the city. Anyway you can eat rats, in some countries they are a delicacy. So set up a few spring loaded rat-traps and hopefully you will have something to eat. You have to be careful with rats as they carry disease so you do not want to get bitten. That is why the spring loaded rat-traps are probably better. I've never cooked a rat before but according to my survival manual you wrap the dead rat in mud or clay and put it in the fire and leave it. The next day or after it has cooled down you break open the baked mud covering and it should be ready to eat. The fur and skin should be stuck in the mud and the guts should be all shriveled up. This way you don't need to skin them or gut them. Just a thought.

When you are in the countryside things are very different because you will be exposed so I would keep off the roads. And I think there will be less empty house because as people have moved out of the cities they will have moved into the closest houses. So you will need to scout around until you have found a number of empty houses that you can slowly move your things into. Then when you are tired of moving you can look for your new home. Now everything you have learned in the city still applies. Keep all your goodies well hidden so if anyone raids your place you don't lose everything.So the first thing you do when you get to a new house is to start hiding things you are not using. And I mean hiding and that could mean in the house next door or in a pile of rubbish out the back. I don't like everything in one place because of the mobs and also because of fire. We are back to using fire so expect the possibility of something catching on fire. Also fire and smoke is a signal and will draw people to you so if you do not want to meet the locals keep the smoke out of site. And that could mean cooking in a forest or away from where you are living.

Now if you have to move in a hurry, what do you take? If you are walking around with a brand new backpack filled to the hilt, you are going to be a target. And you don't want that. There are many "Get out of Dodge" bags or survival kits or whatever you call them. But if you have to leave in a hurry on foot what do you do. Now you might have to move because the meandering mobs are taking over or an uncontrollable fire is sweeping into your neighborhood. After society collapses and clean water gets hard to find then I expect water borne diseases to thin out the population. So I hope the meandering mobs get thinned out. But don't bet on it, as they will take all the clean water supplies.

Now if you have to leave in a hurry I would bury or hide any good stuff just in case you make it back. This way if you move a couple of hours away you can still come back. But if you are not coming back and you have to run then this is what I would take. At the moment I am putting bleach in smaller, flat plastic bottles like shampoo bottles and skin care bottles. These small flat plastic bottles I can distribute them around in my pockets and bag. I'm also stocking up on heavy-duty baggy pants with lots of pockets and I'm getting extra pockets sown on the inside for hidden goodies like bleach and fishing gear. The most important items you need are: something to purify water and something to catch food with. So in your hidden pockets you need fishing line and hooks and if you can a very good rat-trap or two and spring loaded traps are flat. After society collapses there will be lots of rats and that is what you will live off until you get established.

Bleach or something to purify water with is the most important. Because we cannot live too long without water and after two days without water you will possibly have trouble thinking straight. You need water so water is number one. Next comes food and that is how to catch food while you are on the run. I would stock up on heavy-duty rat traps, spring loaded. They have been around for a long time so they are very effective. You'll need a number of these. Also fishing line and many hooks. Here again buy the best quality as they will last the longest. Next is fire. That means a flint and steel, a magnifying glass or even a cigarette lighter. You need to be able to start a fire. Next, comes the seeds. You should carry as many seeds as you can because they are the future. And I would also plant seeds along the way. This way if you come back hopefully there might be food growing in places.

After the electricity goes off mankind is going from the Information Age to the Stone Age in a very short time. That means you will be a scavenger and a hunter/gatherer until you get settled again. The remnants of hunter/gatherer societies still around nowadays planted gardens in areas they visited, so they knew there was food in several places in their area. You should do the same. Just using The Colony 2 as an example of how much we have forgotten in our modern life. The first or second day after the colonist landed they found fishing gear in one of the boats. It took them over a week to go fishing. They should have put a bug on a hook and thrown a fixed line in that little stream just to see if anything lived there. They could have tired the line to a tree and left it overnight. No sinker just leave the bug on the surface of the water, but the weight of the hook would probably sink it. Use small hooks because a small hook could catch a big fish but a big hook will possible not catch a small fish. I would have done this as soon as I had found the line. Every time we went camping we always threw a line in to see if we could get something to eat. Usually where there is running water there are fish. The colonist went into hunter/gatherer mode, but it took them over a week to do so. They never ate the first snake they killed or used it as bait. And I think most people would do they same. So this is where training your mind comes in. Whenever you stop for the night set up a couple of rattraps, make sure they are tired down. If you are by a stream that doesn't look too polluted, throw a line in and see if you catch breakfast.

Chapter 21

Time Line For Saving Your Family

The problem is nobody knows when the world is going to come unglued. So don't put off starting to plan your future because everything is still pretty rosy. The good times are not going to last forever.

- 1 To start off I'd start saving seeds and throwing them around your area. Seeds are the future and you will need them to survive. Just save the seeds from all the vegetables and fruit you buy and throw them around near where you live. And also dry some out to keep as backups just in case the world comes unglued a bit too early.

- 2 I'd get into making and eating sprouts. This will be a big part of your survival food when things go from bad to very bad. This way you'll know how to grow them and how long they take to grow. You will also know why you need lots of seeds. After things quiet down you will need seeds to start a garden.

- 3 Start looking for hiding places inside and outside your house. You need to have some of your survival items hidden outside just in case your house catches on fire. You don't really need to start hiding anything just yet. You will start to do that just before society collapses. Right now you are just looking for places.

- 4 Start your food storage. That means having a slow walk around the supermarket and seeing what you need. Look for products that are in containers that can be reused. And just buy a little each time you go shopping. Set up a rotation system so you use the older products first.

- 5 Start saving all reusable containers, like plastic bottles and jars and tins, even plastic bags. Anything you can use to store food and other items in, will come in handy when you can't get them any more.

- 6 Make sure you have chlorine bleach in your home just in case. If the water goes off this will save your life. You will also need hydrogen peroxide for sterilizing water and as an antiseptic for cuts and other minor injuries.

- 7 Start buying food like tinned fish and putting it in your food rotation system. I consider tinned fish and chlorine bleach essential items.

- 8 Start turning your backyard from lawn into vegetables. I would do this the slow way because this way the vegetable garden will not get on top of you, and you will be able to keep it under control.

- 9 Start stocking up on essentials that you can store and basically forget about like gear for fishing and sowing needles and thread, plus a Swiss Army Knife or two and a multipurpose tool or two. These will come in handy when you need them.

- 10 Go fishing and camping. You do not need to do the survival thing just yet, just learn how to have fun away from the city.

- 11 Start looking at possible places to go to just in case your hometown becomes a war zone. As population pressures mount there will be strife in large cities so be prepared to get out. There has already been strife in some cities in Asia and the Middle East so keep that in mind. If you stay you could put your life and your family's life in danger. When looters destroy your house they will probably set it on fire. That is why you will need stashes of food and survival equipment stored outside your house. Possibly buried in your back yard so you can go back and get it later.

- 12 Learn new skills and buy books. When the electricity goes off you will lose everything on your computer so books are a must. You need books on how to live without a doctor, how to grow things and how to live without electricity. Books are very important. Get a book on plants you can eat and know which plants are not safe. Or get the information off the internet and when things start to break down print it all off. I have a back up hard drive with all my survival information on it. Whenever I have some free time I print off a bit. When I am copying from the internet I copy and paste into Notepad and this way I remove all the formatting. And I can put a lot more information on one page. Do the same with pdf files. This way you can copy paste only the information you need to know.

- 13 Find like-minded people. There are people out there just like you and you should try and meet up with them. I went to a "How to turn your lawn into food" hands on weekend course and I met a number of people who were learning how to survive the future. And that is what you should be doing, getting out there and meeting people.

Documentaries, Books and Magazines Mentioned

The Biblehttp://bibleresources.bible.com/
bible_kjv.php

http://www.energypulse.net/centers/article/
article_display.cfm?a_id=2323

http://news.discovery.com/archaeology/nazca-
civilization-collapse-trees.html

http://ngm.nationalgeographic.com/2008/09/soil/
bourne-text

http://www.guardian.co.uk/world/2009/jul/12/india-
water-supply-bhopal

http://www.guardian.co.uk/society/2010/aug/12/the-
end-of-antibiotics-health-infections

http://www.google.com/hostednews/ap/article/
ALeqM5gmy8vp2IF0hXIS66YjPRglOJg52QD9HR
VQF80

http://www.thestandard.com.hk/news_detail.asp?
pp_cat=11&art_id=102958&sid=29587235&con_ty
pe=1&d_str=20100915&sear_year=2010

This link is to an article about diet and polio by
Benjamin P. Sandler, M.D.
 http://www.whale.to/v/sandler.html

This article is about how baking soda was used
during the 1918 flu quite successfully to stop the
flu.

http://www.lewrockwell.com/orig5/mercola21.1.ht
ml

This link is to a government site telling you how to
purify water using
bleach
http://www.doh.wa.gov/phepr/handbook/purify.htm

How to purify water using Hydrogen Peroxide
http://www.inspectapedia.com/water/
Drinking_Water_Purification5.htm

How to make soap from scratch
http://www.thefarm.org/charities/i4at/surv/
soapmake.htm

This link here is about how to make your own butter
http://www.positron.org/food/butter/

http://www.rodaleinstitute.org/files/
FSTbookletFINAL.pdf

Reverend Thomas Malthus's "Essay on the
Principle of Population"

http://www.constitution.org/cmt/malthus/
population.htm
http://www.biw.kuleuven.be/aee/clo/idessa_files/
Malthus1798.pdf

Dr. Albert A. Bartlett's "Arithmetic, Population, and Energy"
http://www.albartlett.org/presentations/
arithmetic_population_energy.html

Gerard Diamond Guns Germs and Steel
Collapse: How Societies Choose to Fail or Succeed

Erich Von Daniken Chariots of the Gods Video
Why Egypt Fell - National Geographic
Life After People - History Channel
Mega Structures
Modern Marvels
Ancient Apocalypses - BBC
After Armageddon
http://www.imdb.com/title/tt1607542/

The Colony 1 and 2

Gerard Diamond's Collapse on National Geographic
Earth 2100

What the Romans Did For Us
http://en.wikipedia.org/wiki/
What_the_Romans_Did_for_Us

Civilization: A Personal View by Kenneth Clark
Six Degrees Could Change The World
Survivorman
Man v Wild
Filthy Rich and Homeless

Peak Oil
The Power of Community - How Cuba Survived
Peak Oil
How The Earth Changed History
BBC History Cold Case

Movies That May Have Influenced This Book

Memories of a Survivor
Panic in Year Zero
2012

The Future Will Be Here Sooner Than You Think

I can't see the planet surviving too much longer. I'm giving it four years but even that might be too long. This economic crisis we are in now is not going to go away. We have to adapt to a different future, a future where there is not too much of everything. I don't know what is going to go first, it could be the bees, or oil or a severe El Nino event could wreak havoc on parts of the planet. Something has got to give and when it does you'll be glad you stocked up on the seeds and the sprouting dishes.

What you do now is up to you, but if you want to find out more about how to come to terms with the future check out the website http://www.animalsdinosaursandbugs.com/The-Future.htm and click over to the blog and have your say. As long as the electricity keeps going we will have the internet, so we can keep in touch. But we can only do that as long as there is electricity. So until the electricity stops, and all we need for that to happen is a major failure at a big coal fired generating plant, keep in touch and plan for the future.

All The Best For The Future.

Peter Legrove
Our human global society is very fragile:

I'm not an army man nor a survival man. I'm just an everyday type of dude that took an interest in how long our civilization is going to last. I was into peak oil before peak oil became mainstream. I've been following global warming and climate change since it started so I've been waiting and preparing for some drastic changes in the way we live for a long time now.

I'm into gardening, sustainable living and saving seeds. In the spring and summer time I throw seeds around when I go for a walk to see if I can start wild gardens. I've checked out the survival manuals and I'm a great follower of Bear Grills and the Survivorman. As well as Discovery Channel's "I Shouldn't Be Alive" and a few of the other survival type programs. You can pick up some good ideas from them.

But the main thrust of what I'm interested in is history. The Roman Empire and why it went under as well as the other empires and how man has progressed from the cave to where we are now. And how far we are going to go back when things come apart then how long it takes to reinvent the technology we have lost. I'm a great follower of Gerard Diamond and his collapse scenarios due to climate change and guns, germs and steel.

I will look back and try to figure out what actually tipped us over the edge because everyone under 50 years old will see the start. We are going to collapse but we don't know when. This book is about my journey and how I plan to survive the future.

This is a true story it just hasn't happened yet. The planet is changing and it will not be as friendly as to us as it has been for the last 150 odd years. We are out growing our water supply, our food supply, our oil supply and our electricity supply. Something has got to give. We just don't know which one will give first.

I'm an English teacher, I've been teaching English as a Second Language for years now. I lived in Mexico City for a while before the place modernized and before the big Mexico earthquake destroyed the place. I remember lying in bed and every time there was a shake thinking is this the big one. But it happened after I had left. The Mexico City I knew was an amazing place to live in. A huge sprawling overcrowded metropolis that was full of life. After that I moved onto Central America to have a look around.

Somewhere along the line I ended up in Indonesia before it went mad. A combination of collapse and over crowding. When I was there is was a laid back place with very friendly people. I could never understand why it went mad. But I think it might have had something to do the kids. The parents would count off their kids. "This is number one, this is number two" and so on up to number eight and sometimes up to number twelve. There were kids everywhere. I loved that place, probably a combination of being a burnt out hippie in a laid back country. But in the end it came unglued.

Next it was on to a modern overcrowded city that never stopped this was Hong Kong before the Asia financial crisis. And it was the place to be. But the overcrowding and unhealthy living paid a price so I moved over the border to mainland China, before that place went economically mad. There you could live cheap and healthy and they loved learning so I always had a job. I lived there during their economical miracle and the changes were something sort of amazing. I was there for the SARS and that was a bit of a problem but nobody seemed to worry too much about it.

Before Hong Kong used to be the place to be but it was left behind in the dust and pollution coming from the next economic superpower. And China is still growing. It could possibly be the last big country standing with its One Or Two Child Policy, if it still has it, and not being a democracy. They can still feed themselves and they don't use much oil to do it.

More Books By Peter LeGrove About Surviving The Future

<u>Are You Ready For Civilization Collapse</u>

This book is also about what to do when our society comes unglued. It is a prelude to this book and also contains valuable information to survive the coming collapse.

<u>Is Vegetable Gardening For You</u>

If you are new to prepping the first thing you should do is start a vegetable garden and this little book shows you how to start the easy way. And as you get better at gardening you should be on top of your garden and eating what you grow.

<u>Live Cheap In An UnCheap World</u>

To prepare for the future you need to live cheap and this book shows you how to get by on very little. As the world comes unglued you will need to lower your standard of living and hopefully have some money to spare.

How To Get Out of Debt

To survive a collapse it would help to be debt free unless everything collapses and then you would not need to worry but before that happens they will come after what you owe and what you own. There are standard formulas for getting out of debt but you also need to make extra money and this little book shows you how

How to Lose Weight In An Overweight World

To survive the coming collapse you need to be fit and reasonable healthy, and if you are slightly overweight this little book could set you on the path to a healthier future. When the world comes unglued you need to be quite fit as you will be doing more manual work.

All the best for the future

Peter Legrove

plegrove@gmail.com

www.animalsdinosaursandbugs.com

Live Cheap In An UnCheap World

If You Like My Book
Please write a review on Amazon showing your appreciation
How to Write a Review on Amazon
Go to
https://www.amazon.com/dp/B083SJBPR9

- Scroll down to Customer Reviews
- Click on "Write a customer review" and do your thing. As long or as short as you like.

Amazon will then check it and after a while it will be live on Amazon.

Now you can give the book a grade, how many Gold Stars would you like to give the book.

Thank you
Peter LeGrove

DISCLAIMER:
This ebook is for information only.
The information has not been approved by
the FDA, the USDA or any other
governmental regulatory body or the
equivalent in any country.
When our society does come apart you will
be better prepared to survive but I can't
guarantee your future survival.
Dried food is not always safe to eat.
Baking soda and keeping your blood sugar
levels normal have never been scientifically
proven to stop pandemics but then again
neither have vaccines.
Bleach and H2O2 have never been proven to
be a 100% effective against water borne
diseases but they will give you a better
chance of staying alive.
Although the author and publisher have
made every effort to ensure that the
information in this book was correct at press
time, the author and publisher do not assume
and hereby disclaim any liability to any

party for any loss, damage, or disruption caused by errors or omissions, whether such errors or omissions result from negligence, accident, or any other cause.

This book is for entertainment purposes only. The views expressed are of the author alone and should not be taken as expert advice. The reader is responsible for his own actions. Neither the author nor the publisher assume any liability or responsibility on behalf of the reader or purchaser of this material.

You must use common sense after the world collapses. The author and publisher assume no liability or responsibility for any accidents or anything that happens to you while reading or following this book. The author is not a licensed Prepper in any country in the world, he is an author writing about what he did to survive the future.

The author and publisher claim no responsibility for results obtained while following this book, as everybody is different and are starting at different levels. You the reader are responsibility for your actions and safety while trying to stay alive after the SHTF.

9 781660 158898